LOVE
AND THE
MESSIANIC
AGE

PAUL PHILIP LEVERTOFF

MESSIANIC
LUMINARIES
SERIES

LOVE
AND THE
MESSIANIC
AGE

PAUL PHILIP LEVERTOFF

With Introduction, Biography,
Bibliography, and Explanatory Notes

VINE OF DAVID

First Fruits of Zion is a 501(c)(3) registered nonprofit educational
organization.

Vine of David is a publishing arm of the ministry of First Fruits of
Zion dedicated to resurrecting the voices of Messianic pioneers and
luminaries. If you would like to assist in the publication of these voices
from the past you can sponsor the translation and publication their
important works please visit **www.vineofdavid.org** for needs and
opportunities.

**First Edition 1923, Episcopal Hebrew Christian Church
Publications, London.**

Second Edition 2009, Vine of David, USA.

Printed in the United States of America

Republished with the kind permission of the Denise Levertov Literary
Trust, Paul A. Lacey, Valeris Trueblood, co-trustees.

ISBN: 978–1–892124–33–3

Cover Design: Avner Wolff

Vine of David

PO Box 649, Marshfield, Missouri 65706–0649 USA
Phone (417) 468–2741, www.ffoz.org

Comments and questions: www.ffoz.org/contact

Also available from Vine of David:
Love and the Messianic Age: Study Guide and Commentary

First Fruits of Zion: www.ffoz.org
Vine of David: www.vineofdavid.org

CONTENTS

Feivel the Chasid. 1

Introduction: *Love and the Messianic Age*. 11

Preface. 21

Contents 25

"The Search" 27

Chapter 1: Knowledge and Love 31

Chapter 2: The Law and Love 43

Chapter 3: Fear and Love 49

Chapter 4: Joy and Love 55

Chapter 5: Prayer and Love 59

Chapter 6: Repentance and Love 65

Saint Paul's Hymn of Love 71

Epilogue: Love in the Fourth Gospel. .73

"Clasping of Hands". 81

A Selected Bibliography of Levertoff's Published Works 83

PAUL PHILIP LEVERTOFF

פאול פיליפ (פייבל) לברטוב

5639–5714 (1878–1954)

FEIVEL THE CHASID

A BRIEF BIOGRAPHY OF
PAUL P. LEVERTOFF [1]

In 1887 a nine-year-old Chasidic Jew named Feivel Levertoff was trudging home from the *cheder* (a Jewish day school) when a discarded scrap of paper caught his eye. It was printed with Hebrew text. Supposing it was a leaf from a prayer book or other sacred volume, Feivel picked it out of the snow.

He quickly read the piece of paper. It was a page from a book he had never read before. It told the story of a boy like himself—not much older either—whose parents found him in the Holy Temple in Jerusalem, expounding the Scriptures and learning with the great sages of antiquity.

> When they did not find Him, they returned to Jerusalem looking for Him. Then, after three days they found Him in the temple, sitting in the midst of the teachers, both listening to them and asking them questions. And all who heard Him were amazed at His understanding and His answers. (Luke 2:45–47, NASB)

Intrigued, Feivel hurried home and showed the scrap to his father, Shaul Levertoff. To Feivel's surprise, his father was not

---

[1] Adapted from Jorge Quiñónez, "Paul Philip Levertoff: Pioneering Hebrew-Christian Scholar and Leader," *Mishkan* 37 (2002): 21–34. Special thanks to Jorge for his assistance and his dedication to keeping alive the memory of nineteenth-century Jewish believers.

pleased. As soon as he read it, he became angry, crumpled it up and tossed it into the stove. "You must never read such things! If you ever find writings like this again, do not read them," his father ordered. Feivel was puzzled. He had never before seen a Hebrew text destroyed as if it were a scrap from a newspaper. How was he supposed to know the difference between the forbidden words and holy writings if he did not know what the forbidden writings were? He wondered who the wise boy in the story was. Secretly, he wished he had never shown the mysterious fragment to his father.

Feivel was the son of Shaul and Batya Levertoff, a family of Sephardic Jews in Orsha, Belarus. The Levertoff family had strong Chasidic leanings. The Chasidim are a mystical, orthodox sect of Judaism known for their piety, esoteric scholarship, and devotion to God. The Chasidic movement began with the teachings of their charismatic leader, the Baal Shem Tov, in the mid-eighteenth century. Sects of Chasidim are characterized by radical discipleship to a rebbe—a great rabbi and spiritual leader over a community. The disciple of such a rebbe is called a *chasid* (חסיד), a biblical Hebrew word that means "devoted one." In Chasidic Judaism the disciples of a rebbe regard their teacher as a prophet, miracle worker, saint, and intermediary between them and God—a living link to God. A Chasidic rebbe is to his Chasidim like a small version of what Moses was to Israel.

Feivel's family were distant relatives of the famous Rabbi Shneur Zalman of Liadi (1745–1812), the first Lubavitcher rebbe[2] and author of a famous Chasidic treatise called *Likutei Amarim* ("A Collection of Sayings"), also called *Tanya* ("Teaching"). Feivel's great-grandmother was Rabbi Zalman's niece.

True to his prestigious family ancestry, nine-year-old Feivel was already showing signs of becoming a great scholar when he found the scrap from the Gospel of Luke. That explains why

---

[2] In Lubavitch circles, he is also known as the Alter Rebbe, a Yiddish term that means "Old Rebbe" (*Admor HaZaken* [אדמו"ר הזקן] in Hebrew).

he was so intrigued by the mysterious page from the forbidden book.

Some time later Feivel unwittingly came across another Gospel passage—this time from the book of John. Because of John's rich, mystical content, Feivel assumed the text was a Chasidic discourse. When he realized that he had actually been reading the Gospel of John, his curiosity about Christianity and its forbidden books was heightened.

After bar mitzvah at the age of thirteen, Feivel began his formal education at the prestigious Volozhin Yeshiva in Lithuania, where he excelled in his studies and graduated early. He was well on his way to becoming a celebrated rabbi.

He continued his learning at a university in the Prussian city of Königsberg. It was there, at the age of seventeen, that he encountered the Gospels again. Outside of his community and far from home, this time he determined to read them through.

He read the Gospels in German. Then he obtained a Hebrew version and reread them. Though he was in the midst of a Gentile, Christian city where Jesus was worshiped in churches and honored in every home, Feivel felt the Gospels belonged more to him and the Chasidic world than they did to the Gentiles who revered them. He found the Gospels to be thoroughly Jewish and conceptually similar to Chasidic Judaism. He wondered how Gentile Christians could hope to comprehend Yeshua and His words without the benefit of a classical Jewish education or experience with the esoteric works of the Chasidim.

Moreover, the writings led him to a profound and shaking conclusion: Yeshua of Nazareth had indeed been the promised Messiah. From then on, Feivel was the devoted Chasid of Rebbe Yeshua of Nazareth.

When seventeen-year-old Feivel returned home from school, he found himself quickly alienated from his family and community because of his new convictions. He determined to leave his parents—a decision he later regretted, stating that if only he had been wiser he would have been able to persuade his parents, for he realized how near the kingdom they were. In December of 1896 he was baptized into Christianity and took the Christian name Paul Philip. He spent much of the rest of his life living as a lone Chasid in the midst of a Christian world.

Levertoff went on to work as a translator, writer, and evangelist for missionary organizations including the London Jews' Society and the Hebrew Christian Testimony to Israel. He undertook mission trips together with the famous Jewish believer David Baron throughout Europe, to Egypt, and to the Holy Land.

In the first decade of the twentieth century, Levertoff wrote a variety of titles for the mission societies that employed him. He was prolific, often exploring the intersection between the Gospels and Chasidic Judaism. His book about Yeshua, *Ben haAdam, Chayey Yeshua ha-Mashiach uPealav* (*The Son of Man: A Survey of the Life and Deeds of Jesus Christ*), was the first work ever written about Yeshua in modern Hebrew. Other publications included a book on Paul, numerous articles in mission society journals, and translations of Christian books into modern Hebrew.

In 1910 Levertoff took a missions position in Constantinople, where he met Welsh-born Beatrice Spooner-Jones, the woman who became his wife. She bore him two daughters, Olga and Denise. Olga Levertoff went on to become a writer, a devout supporter of proto-Messianic Judaism, and a Jewish-rights activist in England instrumental in bringing about civil rights reform to that country. Denise relocated to America, where she became a celebrated anti-war political activist and famous poet, publishing under the name Denise Levertov.

In a letter to Levertoff from the notable Jewish believer Chaim Yedidiah Pollak,[3] the latter acknowledges that he initially criticized Levertoff for his choice in marriage (a Gentile woman), but had since heard good reports about her: "Herewith I say peace to you and to your [wife], for already you have a [wife], and my dear brother A. Wigand the honorable pastor praises your [wife] very much." Nevertheless, Pollak decried what he perceived to be

---

[3]   Lucky Williams to Levertoff, a hand-written apology in Hebrew, undated, Stanford University Library, Denise Levertov Papers, M0601, Box X, Folder Y. Pollak is also known as Theophilus Lucky.

Levertoff's drift from the halachic Torah standards of Orthodox Judaism:

> I cried out with a great and bitter outcry. For it is a great pain of my soul to see a man like you which the Lord has granted you understanding, knowledge, and wisdom, and you are surely able to be an example to this generation, an example to our generation and to the generations which will come after us. For you possess our language and you can be a writer in Israel. You are created to benefit our people, to open the eyes of the blind, and to show echoes of the glory of the Messiah of the Lord, Yeshua our Master, may His name be blessed for ever and ever. And you turn aside from the way of truth, from the way which the Lord desires that we should walk in it.

By "way of truth," Pollak meant Torah observance as defined by traditional, Orthodox Judaism. To some extent, Pollak's criticism was accurate. Marriage to a Gentile woman was a part of the Christianization trend that shaped Levertoff's life and ministry henceforth. Children born to her would not be legally Jewish. After marriage Levertoff seems to have accepted a more conventional Christian life and practice, even accepting Christian ordination as a member of the Anglican clergy.

In 1912 Levertoff moved to Leipzig, Germany, where he took a position as the professor of Hebrew and rabbinics at the Institutum Judaicum Delitzschianum. The institute was a postgraduate school for Jewish missions, originally founded by Franz Delitzsch.[4] Levertoff was filling the post left vacant by the death of the eminent Jewish believer Rabbi Yechiel Tzvi Herschensohn-Lichtenstein. Levertoff taught courses in Yiddish and Hebrew, in Tanach, in rabbinics, and in the Apostolic Writings. He taught from the Hebrew commentaries on the Apostolic Writings written by his predecessor Rabbi Lichtenstein and helped edit the Matthew commentary for publication.

---

[4] Translator of the Delitzsch Hebrew New Testament.

During World War I, he lost his posting at the school and was placed under house arrest for the duration of the war because he was a Russian national. Nevertheless, while under arrest, he was commissioned by the University of Leipzig to write a German translation with commentary of *Pesikta Rabbati* (a medieval collection of midrash), a German translation of the Jerusalem Talmud, and a treatise on Chasidic Judaism titled *Die religiöse Denkweise der Chassidim* (*The Religious Ideas of the Chasidim*). The German *Pesikta Rabbati* was never published but still exists in manuscript form in the Stanford library archives. The University of Leipzig withdrew the commission for the Jerusalem Talmud translation in response to rising German anti-Semitism. Levertoff did complete and publish the third work, *The Religious Ideas of the Chasidim*. Disguised as an inquiry in the field of comparative religion, Levertoff used the opportunity to work out a Christian-Chasidic theology that could be utilized in a community of Jewish believers. The work was influenced by the writings of Levertoff's distant ancestor, Shneur Zalman of Liadi, and Levertoff's own early life and education in the midst of Chasidic Judaism. He later wrote a much shorter English version of the book and released it under the title *Love and the Messianic Age*.

Between the world wars Levertoff moved to Wales, the home country of his wife. He subsequently took a position of leadership in the Church of England. Nevertheless, he longed for an authentic Jewish expression of his faith. In the 1920s he issued a call to Jewish believers in the London area, inviting them to form a Jewish-Christian congregation. Levertoff became the only Anglican priest to conduct services while wearing a tallit and *kippah*, to lead his congregation in the recitation of the *Shema* and traditional Jewish prayers, and to read aloud to the community from a Torah scroll. At Sabbath meals he led the congregation in traditional handwashing before breaking bread and then adorned the meal with Sabbath table songs. A vivid description of the service can be found in *The Wailing Wall* by his daughter

Olga Levertoff.[5] In 1925 he published a Hebrew liturgy for the service called *Meal of the Holy King,* which represents a fusion of the Anglican Church's order of service and traditional synagogue prayers.

Levertoff dreamed of establishing a genuine Messianic expression of Judaism. He wanted to see a congregational movement of similar Hebrew-Christian churches under the auspices of the missionary organization, the International Hebrew Christian Alliance (IHCA). Initially his ideas were well received by the IHCA, but on further reflection they withdrew their support. The Christian missionary movement had difficulty endorsing the idea of Jewish Christians continuing to practice any vestiges of Judaism or Torah.

In the 1930s Levertoff joined a translation team to create an English version of *Zohar* for the Soncino Press. He translated two of the five volumes. In the academic world Levertoff is perhaps most famous for his work on the Soncino English translation of the *Zohar.* The Soncino translation of the *Zohar* is still the most popular English version in circulation today. He also translated an abbreviated version of *Sifre,* an ancient midrash on the books of Numbers and Deuteronomy.

During World War II Levertoff worked for British Intelligence and was active in rescuing Jews from Austria. All the while, he continued to lead Jewish worship services within the Anglican Church.

Levertoff believed that the Gospels and Chasidic Judaism merged seamlessly, and he dedicated his scholarship to demonstrating that conviction. He is said to have best developed his ideas in his major life work, a manuscript on the subject of Christ and the Shechinah. Unfortunately, the book was never published and the manuscript has been lost; however, he presented a lecture titled "The Shekinah Motif in the New Testament Literature" to the Society of the Study of Religions that we may assume represented something of an abstract of the larger

---

5   Olga Levertoff, *The Wailing Wall* (London: A.R. Howbray & Co., 1938), 117–135.

work. This short paper provides a glimpse into a compelling and radical attempt to reconcile Jewish mysticism and faith in an exalted, divine Messiah.

For Messianic Judaism of our own day, Feivel Paul Philip Levertoff is a hero of the previous generation, a trailblazer and luminary ahead of his time. The Lord did indeed grant him understanding, knowledge, and wisdom to be an example to his generation, an example to our generation and to the generations that will come after us. Services in Messianic Jewish congregations today are similar to those Levertoff conducted a generation ago. From the time he first came to Messiah to the end of his life, Levertoff understood that the faith practiced by Yeshua and his followers was Judaism. Though he lived in a Christian world, he did not abandon his convictions about Judaism, his Chasidic roots, or his steadfast belief that the Gospels and Apostolic Writings belonged to Judaism.

Feivel Paul Philip Levertoff died at the age of 75 on July 31, 1954, on *Rosh Chodesh Av* (the New Moon of the fifth month).

Just before his death, Levertoff rose from his bed and danced a joyful Chasidic dance. Meanwhile, "an ocean away" in North America, his younger daughter Denise Levertov, completely oblivious of her father's passing, spontaneously performed a wild dance of mourning and praise, "unaware that he, perhaps at the same moment, had risen from his deathbed at the last to perform a Hasidic dance as well."[6]

> My father danced a Hassidic dance the day
> before he died.
> His daughters they were far away, his wife was
> by his side.

---

[6] Janet Tassel, "Poetic Justice in El Salvador: Denise Levertov Brings Her Poetry and Politics to the Oratorio Form," in *Conversations with Denise Levertov* (ed. Jewel Spears Brooker Jackson; Jackson, MS: University Press of Mississippi, 1998), 126.

He danced for Jesus his Messiah who rose up
    from the dead
And left the tomb for the upper room and was known
    in the breaking of bread.

Except you become as a little child my kingdom
    you shall not see.
So he danced in his joy as he did when a boy
    and as often he danced for me.

He danced for those he left long ago and for those
    he never knew,
For an end of strife for eternal life for behold
    I shall make all things new.

My father danced a Hassidic dance and sang
    with his latest breath.
The dance of peace it will never cease till life
    has conquered death.

My father danced and then he died and his name
    is a long time gone.
His voice was stilled and his task fulfilled for a people
    that shall be born.   (OLGA LEVERTOFF)[7]

May he be remembered for good, and may the publication of
this volume bring honor to his Rebbe, at whose table his soul
still dances.

---

[7]   Olga Levertoff, "The Ballad of My Father," as printed in Denise
Levertov, *The Sorrow Dance* (New York: New Direction Publication
Corporation, 1967), 93–94.

INTRODUCTION

LOVE AND THE MESSIANIC AGE

D. THOMAS LANCASTER

During World War I, as a Russian national in Germany, Paul Philip Levertoff was placed under house arrest for the duration of the war. He made good use of the time. The University of Leipzig commissioned him to write a treatise on Chasidic Judaism. Levertoff took the opportunity to write a study of comparative religion, comparing Chasidic Judaism with the New Testament. The completed work was published in Leipzig by J. C. Hinrichs under the title *Die religiöse Denkweise der Chassidim* (*The Religious Ideas of the Chasidim*).

Ostensibly an academic inquiry in comparative religion, Levertoff's work was actually an attempt on his part to work out a Christian-Chasidic theology that could be utilized in a community of Jewish believers. Moreover, it had subtle, apologetic tones in defense of Chasidic theology.

The work was influenced by the writings of Levertoff's distant ancestor, Shneur Zalman of Liadi, the first Lubavitcher rebbe and founder of the Chasidic dynasty, which resulted in today's Chabad-Lubavitch movement. It was well received. According to daughter Denise Levertov, Martin Buber drew inspiration from

Levertoff's attempt to communicate the Chasidic world—inspiration that resulted in his popular *Tales of the Chasidim*.

Die religiöse Denkweise der Chassidim has not yet been translated to English, but in 1923, Levertoff released a shorter version of the same work in English, titled *Love and the Messianic Age: In hitherto untranslated Hasidic writings; with special reference to the Fourth Gospel*. The English version was published by the Episcopal Hebrew Christian Church in London. It is reprinted here with some minor corrections—edits to make the English more readily accessible to the modern reader—and some additional footnotes for clarification. Footnotes in square brackets have been supplied by Vine of David. An asterisk beside a citation may indicate a reference to an edition from Levertoff's library which is no longer available for verification, or it may indicate some other uncertainty with the citation. Permission to republish the works of Paul P. Levertoff was obtained by kind permission of the Denise Levertov Literary Trust, Paul A. Lacey, Valeris Trueblood, co-trustees. All royalties paid to the heirs of the Levertoff estate.

Love and the Messianic Age compares Chasidic Judaism and its ideologies with those of the apostles, focusing primarily on the Gospel of John. Levertoff says that the mystical and transcendent movement "of Jewish piety has an almost Johannine coloring" yet is nonetheless different from the path set out before us by the Master. In the first six chapters, Levertoff briefly summarizes the complex, esoteric teachings of Chasidic Judaism with only sparse commentary. During the course of those six chapters, the reader will be exposed to a variety of mystical constructs, some of which are inspiring and insightful and some of which may seem dubious. It is not necessary to agree with or endorse the mystical concepts Levertoff advances in these chapters. He is merely presenting those concepts as they are taught in Chasidic Judaism for the purpose of comparison and contrast with apostolic theology. Levertoff's method invites the reader to withhold judgment until the epilogue, when he takes us into the book of John. In a series of rapid citations from the words of Yeshua, he demonstrates what could be called a mystical-Chasidic thrust behind those words.

The focus of the work is on the concept of love—love for God and love of fellow as expressed in Chasidic thought and the words of Yeshua. Love for God is bound up with the experience of knowing God and fearing God, relationship to His Torah, and a life characterized by joy, prayer, and repentance. In other words, this is a book about how we experience God and godliness in this world and the Messianic Age to come.

Chasidic thought looks forward to the revelation and consummation of relationship with God in the Messianic Age and encourages us to strive toward experiencing that revelation and consummation in this age. Similarly, faith in Yeshua expresses the future consummation of that relationship of love now in the person of Messiah. Levertoff concludes that the difference between this love as expressed in Judaism and Christianity "is not a difference of degree, but of quality, a difference between expectation and realization."

Levertoff opens *Love and the Messianic Age* with some brief remarks concerning the purpose and nature of the work. He intends "to prove that traditional Orthodox Judaism has no lack of spiritual fervor." By "spiritual fervor" he suggests to his readers that Judaism is not void of charismatic feeling and spirituality as the Christian stereotype assumes. Levertoff wants his readers to feel and experience their relationship with God.

Love and the Messianic Age is an important book for both Messianic Judaism and Christianity. It opens a field of inquiry and reflection that encourages the reader to internalize the spiritual truths of theology and our faith in Messiah. Levertoff leads his readers to consider their relationship with God, their motivations for serving Him, and how their interaction with God and Torah can be expressed in a heart of joy, acts of love, fervent prayer, and sincere repentance. Most importantly, Levertoff's work demonstrates just how mysterious and wonderful the gospel message actually is.

Readers may find the material difficult because it often deals with large, abstract theological concepts in a short summary form. Levertoff's language is academic and densely packed.

To assist readers in unlocking the contents of *Love and the Messianic Age*, Vine of David has prepared an accompanying study guide that can be purchased through the ministry. The academic tone of the first chapter may be particularly discouraging to readers unfamiliar with scholarly discourse, so we encourage you to push through to the subsequent chapters, where you will find the content shorter and more manageable.

The reader who feels wary of a book that so liberally cites mystical Jewish literature will do well to remember that the apostolic faith as expressed in the Gospels, Epistles, and Revelation is also a mystical expression of Judaism. Again, one should keep in mind that the various ideas and concepts presented in the first six chapters need not be accepted at face value. Instead, Levertoff simply presents them for purposes of comparison and contrast with the teachings of Yeshua and the apostles. When studying the Talmud, Midrash, and other Jewish sources, it is not necessary to endorse the whole gamut of the literature to profit immensely from its content. The study of Jewish mysticism is no exception to that rule. Read it, consider it, and then take it or leave it. In any case, Levertoff is a safe and reliable guide in the strange and sometimes unsettling paths of esoteric Jewish thought and theology.

STUDIES IN JEWISH AND CHRISTIAN PIETY.

I. Love
and the
Messianic Age

in hitherto untranslated Hasidic writings;
with special reference to the Fourth Gospel.

BY

REV. PAUL P. LEVERTOFF, M.LITT.,

DIRECTOR OF JEWISH WORK IN CONNECTION WITH THE BISHOP OF STEPNEY'S FUND;

Examiner in Heb., and O.T. Theology for the University of Leeds; late Subwarden
of S. Deiniol's Library, Hawarden; and sometimes Prof. of Heb.
and Aramaic at the Delitzsch Coll., Leipzig.

Author of—

"The Son of Man"; "The Life of S. Paul"; "Israel's Religion and Destiny";
"St. Augustine's Confessions" (in Hebrew); "The
Religious Ideas of Hasidism"; "O.T. Prophecy
and the Religions of the East;"
Contributor to the "International Standard Biblical Ency," etc.

EPISCOPAL HEBREW CHRISTIAN CHURCH PUBLICATIONS,

33, BEDFORD SQUARE,

LONDON, W.C.

TO
MY FATHER

"AN ISRAELITE INDEED IN WHOM THERE IS NO GUILE."

"The peoples of all other nations but the Jewish seem to look backwards and also to exist for the present; but in the Jewish scheme everything is prospective and preparatory; nothing, however trifling, is done for itself alone, but all is typical of something yet to come." (Samuel Taylor Coleridge[8])

"There were two other characteristic marks of their [Israel's] religion: one was their extraordinary and quite unexpected abhorrence of any attempt to represent the Deity in an image, and the other the belief that though they could not make any likeness of God, yet eventually, when men were ready for it, He would give them that which perhaps we may be not far wrong in saying that they somehow vaguely and indefinitely felt would be 'the Image of the Invisible God,' 'the Brightness of His Glory, and the express Image of His Person.'" (Canon W. H. G. Holmes, "The Presence of God"[9])

"Oh that thou wouldest rend the heavens, that thou wouldest come down." (Isaiah 64:1)

---

[8] [Poet and philosopher (1772–1834). One of the founders of the "Romantic Movement" in England.]

[9] [*The Presence of God: A Study in Divine Immanence and Transcendence* (New York: Macmillan, 1923), 24.]

PREFACE

This little book forms the basis of lectures on "Chasidic Teaching in the Light of the New Testament" delivered by me in 1920 before the Origen Society, Lincoln College, Oxford, and at the Community of the Resurrection, Mirfield.

The Hebrew and Aramaic writings[10] on which this treatise is based have never been translated into any language,[11] nor has any

---

[10] Apart from the *Zohar* and other medieval books, I have used chiefly the following sources: Rabbi Schneur Zalman of Liadi, *Tanya* (Slavita: 1797); *Likkutei Torah*; *Torah Or* (Shitomir: 1848); Rabbi Dov Ber of Mezeritch, *Kuntras Hahitpa'alut*; *Shnei HaMeorot* (Königsberg: 1831); Rabbi Aaron HaLevi of Barcelona, *Sha'arei HaYichud Ve'emunah*; *Sha'arei Avodah* (Shklov: 1820–21).

[11] [Since the original publication of *Love and the Messianic Age,* several of Levertoff's "in hitherto untranslated" sources have been translated to English: Rabbi Schneur Zalman, *Tanya* (Brooklyn: Kehot Publication Society, 1972); Rabbi Bachya ben Joseph ibn Paquda, *Chovot HaLevavot* (*Duties of the Heart*) (2 vols.; Jerusalem: Feldheim, 1970); Rabbi Chayim Vital's *Etz Chayim*, ongoing, *The Tree of Life* (New York: Arizal Publications, 2008–present); Rabbi Moshe Cordovero, *Tomer Devorah* (*The Palm Tree of Devorah*) (Southfield: Targum Press, 1993) and *Tomer Devorah* (Jerusalem: Tomer Publications, 2005); *Ramban Nachmanides Commentary on the Torah* (5 vols.; Brooklyn, NY: Shilo Publishing House, 1974). Selections from several of Levertoff's primary sources can be found published as individual discourses in the *Chasidic Heritage Series* (Brooklyn: Kehot Publication Society, 2001–present); *Torah Or* and *Likkutei Torah* are in the process of being made available in English translation by Rabbi Yitzchok Dovid Wagshul and published by the Purity Press. The first two installments in the series are available as: *Words of the Living G-d: Torah Or, Volume One: The Book of Genesis* (New York: Purity Press, 2007) and *Beyond All Reason: Purim Discourse from Torah Or, "Chayav Inash Livsumei"* (Houston: Dwelling Place Publishing, 2006).]

Jewish or Christian scholar ever attempted to reproduce the religious ideas and ideals contained in them. In fact, the style of these writings, their crude coloring and mixture of rabbinical casuistry and Kabbalistic symbolism, their strained efforts at describing what Walter Pater calls "the sensuous love of the unseen," all but defy translation.[12] The writers plunge the reader into a welter of ideas, strung together in sentences three pages long, out of which he at last emerges excited and breathless.

In dealing with any mystical movement in religion—especially in Judaism—one is inclined to follow the method of the German philosopher Jakob Brucker,[13] who began his *Critical History of Philosophy* (1742) with a long description of the *philosophia barbarica* [Latin: "barbarian philosophy"], the first part of which is the *philosophia antediluviana* [Latin: "philosophy of the pre-flood age"].

I would fain enlarge upon the genesis and history of the mystic side of rabbinic Judaism, but for this I may refer the reader to my book on Chasidism,[14] where also I have attempted to prove that these religious conceptions throw some light on the New Testament writings. In any case, these ideas result from the culmination and not the inception of Jewish group mysticism and eschatology. Many thought-forms appearing at the first glance as new I have tried to trace back through medieval Kabbalah, Philo, and early rabbinic, to the pre-Christian Apocalyptic literature.

Christians, in spite of the vast stores of literature available today on Judaism, are generally of the same mind as Dr. Johnson, who, in the famous dictionary, thus defines *Pharisaical*:

---

12 [Walter Horatio Pater, *Plato and Platonism* (London: Macmillan, 1910), 143.]

13 [Johann Jakob Brucker lived in Germany (1696–1770). He was an ordained minister and a historian of philosophy.]

14 *Die religiöse Denkweise der Chassidim (The Religious Ideas of the Chasidim)*(Leipzig: J. C. Hinrichs, 1918).

Pharisaical, adj. (from *Pharisee)* ritual: externally religious: from the sect of the Pharisees, whose religion
consists almost wholly in ceremonies.[15]

But, as Dr. Claude Montefiore says in his *The Old Testament
and After*:

Jewish critics of Christianity and Christian critics of
Judaism make precisely the same charges against each
other. The Christian says: "Judaism thinks of nothing
but reward. It is a low and selfish religion." The Jew says:
"Christians think of nothing but saving their own souls.
Christianity is a self-regarding and selfish religion." Yet
one set of critics is as wrong as the other.[16]

I hope by means of this short study to prove that traditional
Orthodox Judaism has no lack of spiritual fervor.[17] Even "the sea
of the Talmud" has its Gulf Stream of mysticism.[18]

---

[15] [Samuel Johnson, *A Dictionary of the English Language* (1755). It is
one of the most influential dictionaries in the history of the English
language.]

[16] [Claude G. Montefiore, *The Old Testament and After* (London:
Macmillan, 1923), 179–180.]

[17] The terms most frequently used in these writings are:

Achdut [Unity, אחדות]: not only for the divine unity, but also in the
sense of *unio mystica* [Latin: "mystical union"] in relation to God, and
fellowship in relation to man.

Kavanah [כונה]: intention, especially at prayer and in performing
religious duties.

Ahavah [אהבה]: love.

Hitdavkut [התדבקות]: cleaving to God.

Hitpa'allut [התפעלות]: enthusiasm, ecstasy.

Bittul hayesh [בטול היש]: ceasing to be, absorption in God.

For similar terms in the "Mystery Religions" cf. Professor A. Kennedy,
St. Paul and the Mystery Religions (New York: Hodder, 1913), 31–67
and Professor Heinrici, *Die Hermes-Mystik und das Neue Testament*
(Leipzig: Research Institute Publications, 1918).

[18] Cf. Dr. Abelson's interesting book, *Immanence of God in Rabbinic
Literature* (London: Macmillan, 1912), and Kennedy, *St. Paul and the
Mystery Religions*, 31–67.

The reading of the Law and the Prophets in synagogal worship and the liturgical use of the Psalms, have preserved balance in institutional Judaism. On the one hand, it has preserved some groups from a mere formalism, and on the other, from a type of mysticism which is individualistic and anti-social. The strong sense of the divine transcendence has preserved the balance against the danger of pantheism.[19]

But: Δειξαι εκ συγκρισεως το διαφορον … ["To demonstrate the difference by comparison … ," *Deixai ek sugkriseos to diaphoron*].

For, although the trend of this type of Jewish piety has an almost Johannine coloring, the atmosphere of the New Testament is a totally different one.

Christianity is too majestic to live upon the depreciation of rivals. It is the author's hope that Jewish readers of this little book will realize that the difference between Chasidic and Christian conceptions of love is not a difference of degree but of quality, a difference between expectation and realization:

> "And the Word became flesh and dwelt in us (εν ημιν [*en hemin*])." (John 1:14)

St. Matthew's Day, 1923
Holy Trinity Church
Old Nichol Street, Shoreditch

---

[19] [The belief that God is everything and everything is God.]

CONTENTS

Preface.

I.   KNOWLEDGE AND LOVE.

II.   THE LAW AND LOVE.

III.   FEAR AND LOVE.

IV.   JOY AND LOVE.

V.   PRAYER AND LOVE.

VI.   REPENTANCE AND LOVE.

Epilogue: Love in the Fourth Gospel.

"THE SEARCH" [20]

Whither, O whither art Thou fled,
    My Lord, my Love?
My searches are my daily bread,
    Yet never prove.

My knees pierce th' earth, mine eies the skie;
    And yet the sphere
And centre both to me denie
    That Thou art there.

Yet can I mark how herbs below
    Grow green and gay,
As if to meet Thee they did know,
    While I decay.

Yet can I mark how starres above
    Simper and shine,
As having keyes unto Thy love,
    While poore I pine.

I sent a sigh to seek Thee out
    Deep drawn in pain,
Wing'd like an arrow; but my scout
    Returns in vain.

---

20 [George Herbert, *The Temple: Sacred Poems* (London: Seeley and Company, 1906), 204–206. Herbert was a famous Welsh Anglican priest and poet (1593–1633).]

I turn'd another—having store—
       Into a grone,
Because the search was dumbe before;
       But all was one.

Lord, dost Thou some new fabrick mold
       Which favour winnes,
And keeps Thee present; leaving th' old
       Unto their sinnes?

Where is my God? what hidden place
       Conceals Thee still?
What covert dare eclipse Thy face?
       Is it Thy will?

O let not that of anything;
       Let rather brasse,
Or steel, or mountains be Thy ring,
       And I will passe.

Thy will such an intrenching is
       As passeth thought:
To it all strength, all subtilties
       Are things of nought.

Thy will such a strange distance is
       As that to it
East and West touch, the poles do kisse,
       And parallels meet.

Since, then, my grief must be as large
       As in Thy space,
Thy distance from me; see my charge,
       Lord see my case.

O take these barres, these lengths away;
    Turn and restore me:
"Be not Almightie," let me say,
    "Against, but for me."

When Thou dost turn, and wilt be neare,
    What edge so keen,
What point so piercing can appeare
    To come between?

For as Thy absence doth excell
    All distance known,
So doth Thy nearnessse bear the bell,
    Making two one.

(GEORGE HERBERT, 1631)

1

KNOWLEDGE AND LOVE

Mysticism in theology differs from perspectives which are more scientifically logical. Mysticism differs from the logical in the very attitude it takes up in regard to its subject matter at the outset. In rational theology the orderly arrangement of differing ideas permits the selection of some and the rejection of others to harmonize all the units of doctrine. Rational theology organizes these units of doctrine into a comprehensive and more or less self-consistent whole. Rational theology distrusts the irrational absurdity. Mystical theology distrusts the theological perspective which rejects the irrational absurdity as long as life retains the irrational.

The paramount difference between the two begins at the outset, when each defines its sources of knowledge concerning the relations between God and man. The records of religious literature [i.e., Scripture], for instance, enshrine the results of interaction between God and man. Nature also is stamped with a revelation which he who runs may read. To the rational, systematic theologian, evidence such as this, when considered with cool and balanced judgment, affords an opportunity for testing and selecting, approving or disapproving, the value of subjective religious experiences—experiences registered in the heat of individual religious striving today. Reduced to their simplest form, these subjective experiences may be regarded as valid only if they are brought within the field of objective data.

To the mystic, it is not the subjective that has to be viewed in the light of the objective. Rather the historical experience and, so to speak, external religious data has no important value, except as it is caught up into the realm of subjective experience and found to have affinity therewith. The actual feeling, the excitement, has essential value to the mystic. From his perspective, once the experience has been passed into the crucible of conceptual thought and the emotional side of it has been neutralized, it has also been largely sterilized. The two perspectives disagree over the value to be assigned to the personal equation in religious experience.

In the Chasidic theology, now brought under view, this disagreement is clearly illustrated. There are two kinds of knowledge, it is said. On the one hand there is knowledge of God which anyone may acquire by studying creation and acquainting themselves with the character imprinted thereon. On the other hand there is knowledge of the inner being of God. This latter is a progressive knowledge of God. It leads to love of Him, and love for Him brings as its final result the actual vision of Him. To attain this vision—the actual sight of God—is the highest aim; it is a consummation which will not be reached until the Messianic Age, but it is surely promised then. In this connection the prophetic utterances, Deuteronomy 32:39 ("*Behold* that I am He") and Isaiah 40:5 ("All flesh shall *see* together"), are produced to show that the actual vision of God—the beatific vision—is promised under the Mosaic, and will be achieved under the Messianic, dispensation.[21] It is the business of the Chasid to live now for the realization of this Messianic Age.

---

[21] *Torah Or*, Genesis, 16b and often; *Shnei HaMeorot* 9–11*; cf. b.*Pesachim* 68a; b.*Sanhedrin* 91b; *Zohar* I, 87b. When Philo describes "allegory" as dear to ορατικοις ανδρασιν [*oratikois andrasin*], "men of vision" (*Concerning Noah's Work as a Planter* 36), it is unnecessary to believe with Richard Reitzenstein, *Die hellenistischen Mysterionreligionen* (Leipzig: B.G. Teubner, 1910), that the term was borrowed from the "Mystery Religions."

"Love for the Lord is glorious wisdom. To those to whom He appears He gives it, *in order that they may behold Him*" (*Wisdom of Ben Sira* 1:11 [variant textual addition]).

The two forms of knowledge, which we may call the static (i.e., the rational) and the dynamic (i.e., the mystic, productive of the Messianic Age) can be contrasted by means of illustrations. The picture is not the artist, nor is the voice of a singer the personality of the man. We may admire the artist because of the picture, the singer because of the voice, but we do not really know either man. The essence of a man's personality is revealed to the world in the form of holiness and love. In an infinitely higher degree all this is true of God. Creation is merely His picture. It is in knowledge of Himself that true knowledge consists. We know God best when we know Him in His holiness and wisdom and love, apart from His creation. Only Moses had, to some extent, this vision; yet it is the business of all to try and reach this stage.[22]

These writers make no pretence that this outlook which they are commending is easy to attain. In this respect they stand on the same ground as Philo:

> There is nothing better than to search after the true God, even if the finding of Him should escape human capacity, seeing that even eagerness of desire to understand Him in itself produces unspeakable pleasure and delight.
> (*The Special Laws* 1:36)

Another illustration is as follows: There is a difference between him who is eager to see the king and him who is not. The first wanders through the king's palace and realizes its beauty and rejoices in it, even though his wish to see the king himself remains unsatisfied. The other is deprived even of the vision of the *palace*.

However, it is characteristic of him who longs to see the King and to be received by Him, that he keeps himself undefiled and walks in His way.[23]

The knowledge of God which the Chasid thus seeks to cultivate belongs, strictly speaking, to the Messianic world to come.

---

[22] *Likkutei Torah* 59*.

[23] *Shomer Emunim* 15*. Cf. 1 John 3:2–4.

A great deal of Chasidic thought revolves around the consideration of the Messianic Age, which the theologians endeavor, by their method, to anticipate as far as may be. In the Messianic Age the knowledge of God will no longer be merely intellectual apprehension but actual realization in experience.[24]

The present age is a time of pregnancy. The child, the people of God, is in the mother's womb; its breathing organs, which are organs for the reception of God's spirit, are still without function. This embryonic life is the period of Israel's exile. "Rachel weeps for her children" (Jeremiah 31:15) means: The mother of Israel weeps because the Shechinah has departed ("we—*einenu* [איננו]—He—God—is not," can be read as "He has departed").[25] *The Messianic Age will be a time of spiritual birth and growth.*[26] The Messianic days are days in which all creation, even the very animal world, will know God as in days before the fall. The Messianic revelation will be more perfect than the revelation at Sinai. Then it was but momentary, a glimpse; in the new age it will be permanent and continuous. *All we see now is the mirrored reflection;*[27] *then it will be the reality that we see. The least in those days shall be greater than the greatest of these.*[28]

The knowledge which these writers seek to inculcate is, therefore, the knowledge of God's inner essence. It is not attained by processes of rational thinking but by cultivation of immediate

---

[24]   Similarly επιγνωσις ["knowledge," *epignosis*] in 2 Peter 1:8 is regarded both as the root and the end of spiritual progress.

[25]   [The Hebrew word "*einenu* (איננו)" in Jeremiah 31:15 is ambiguous enough that the passage could be translated as "Rachel is weeping for her children … because we are no more" or as "Because He is no more." Levertoff's mystical sources follow this second reading to suggest that Rachel weeps because the Shechinah has departed into exile with Israel.] See *Zohar* III, 20b. It is probable that a similar allegorical interpretation is at the back of Matthew 2:17–18.

[26]   *Torah Or*, Exodus, 139ff.*

[27]   The same metaphor is used as 1 Corinthians 13:12. Also Philo uses εσοπτρον ["mirror," *esoptron*] in the sense that in the mirror we see not the thing itself but only a reflection. Cf. *On Abraham* 153 and often.

[28]   *Shnei HaMeorot* 11*; *Torah Or*, Exodus, 106*; *Sha'arei HaTeshuvah* 8b*.

fellowship with God under discipline to His Spirit. Though we see but the mirrored reflection, we already appreciate the salient fact that God loves us, and upon the basis of this, knowledge of the inner being of God is built. The history of the divine dealings with Israel signifies this one thing: God knows and loves His people.

Great must be the love of the King who stoops to a poor man, freeing him from his misery and bringing him to the palace, and there manifesting to him love and friendship. Thus God deals with Israel. Israel is God's poor man. Out of this little world He has chosen the people of Israel and united Himself with her.[29] It is divine love which runs like a gold thread through history from the very creation of the world itself.

In His relations with man on earth, God has shown Himself a king who desires to make His abode with us here below. The higher a being, the lower he is able to condescend. God wished to be among the small and despised, not as a sultan ruling in his palace, hidden and ruling only by power, but as a good and wise king whose one desire is to draw his subjects to himself; a king who also, out of love for his own, forsakes his palace and dwells among his people in order to unite himself with them, that they may see more of his glory and learn more of his character.[30]

Creation, indeed, signifies of God's perfection. In creation God has *by an act of self-limitation* created conscious beings, that these may have the joy, first, of realizing their selfhood, and then, of realizing Him, their Creator, and of receiving Him into their innermost life as their Father and King. The proof of God's love lies less in the fact that He raises creatures to Himself, than in *that He stoops to have His tabernacle among men* and thus reveal Himself to them. A beautiful simile illustrates this point. It is as though a man accompanied by his young son were climbing a mountain. As the father reaches the summit, he turns to find that the son is far below. But they can still see one another. The son longs to reach the father, but the higher he rises, the more

---

[29]   *Keter Shem Tov*, 8*; *Tanya* 41, 46 and often.

[30]   *Torah Or* 17*; *Chanah Ariel* 16* and often; cf. *Numbers Rabbah* 10:1; *Song of Songs Rabbah* 5:16.

strenuous becomes the task. What does the father do when he sees the intense desire on the part of the son to come to him? He can restrain himself no longer, but comes down to meet him. Even so does God in answer to the strivings of the mystic soul. In this connection, Isaiah 43:7 is interpreted as a figure of God's condescending love.[31]

The two types of knowledge are further illustrated by a reference to the fact that the prophets always compare the ideal wonders of the Messianic Age with the wonders of divine providence in the deliverance of Israel from Egypt, rather than with the wonders of divine power in creation. The great significance of the redemption from Egypt is not the revelation of God's power but of His condescending love for Israel. The illustration of this is as follows. A king invited the representative men of his land to a royal banquet. The rarest dishes were provided, and the guests might help themselves at will. One among the guests there was, however, for whom the king cherished feelings of especial love. For this guest the king selected a portion from one of the simplest dishes and, placing it on a golden platter, *carried it himself to his friend.*

God's dealings with Israel have been ever of this sort.[32]

The "Fathers"—Abraham, Isaac, and Jacob—are called "the chariots of God." [33] Hence, every Israelite is supposed to possess two souls:[34] a "divine" soul, which comes directly from God Himself, and a "natural" or "animal" soul, which comes from the "other side" of God.[35] Israel is called the "son of God," for "as even the toes of the child have their origin in the parents," so has the "divine" soul, even of a sinner, its origin in God; it emanates from Him and unites itself with man's "natural" soul in order to

---

[31] Cf. *Likkutei Torah*, Leviticus, 25c.

[32] *Shnei HaMeorot* 39*. A similar parable in *Mechilta* on Exodus 14:6.

[33] *Genesis Rabbah* 69:3, 82:6. Cf. St. Ignatius, *Epistle to Ephesians* 9: "So ye are all *God-bearers.*"

[34] "And the *souls* which I have made," Isaiah 57:16, is interpreted in this sense.

[35] Exodus 33:23: "And thou shalt see my *back*" is allegorized to express this.

spiritualize it. "It descends from the heights of Heaven, in order to ascend," after having changed the natural into the divine, the material into the spiritual.[36] The metaphor of the "grain of wheat" (see John 12:24) is often used to illustrate the working of this "divine" soul. As the grain must enter into the earth in order to bring forth fruit, so must this soul enter into man's innermost nature and be quite absorbed by it, if it is to bring forth spiritual fruit.

But, as the earth must first be plowed and prepared, so must the natural man be prepared for the divine seed, if this which is hidden in him is to be revealed in all its power.

When the sower sows the seed he is not certain whether it will enter deeply into the ground. When the harvest comes, he rejoices. ("They that sow in tears shall reap in joy."[37]) In the Messianic Age, the time of harvest,[38] all the secrets of human life will be revealed and the achievements of the "divine soul" in every individual will come into the light. At present we are not certain whether it is attaining full fruition. It all depends upon the receptiveness of the human personality and whether it has proved a fertile soil in which the heavenly seed can develop. If the heart of a man has not been broken[39] and if his natural life has not become a vessel of God's love, the "divine element" has not been able to work out its full purpose. His righteousness will lead him to absolute isolation, for it will be mere *self*-righteousness. But if he lets God's love work in him, he can come to such close fellowship with God as to be completely united with Him. As the members of the body are organs of the soul and as the "Angel of the Lord"

---

[36] For the double entity of the soul cf. Aphraates, *Homilies* 6:14. The idea of man possessing several spirits is suggested in the *Testament of the Twelve Patriarchs*, cf. *Testament of Reuben* 3; *Testament of Simeon* 2ff.; *Testament of Judah* 14; cf. *Etz Chayim* 50:2*; *Sha'ar HaKedushah* 3:2*; *Tanya* 1–2. Deuteronomy 32:9: "For the Lord's portion is His people" is thus interpreted "The divine soul of an Israelite *is a part of God Himself*." Cf. *Reshit Chokmah*, section "Fear" 9–10*.

[37] [Psalms 126:5.]

[38] Cf. John 4:35–38.

[39] Cf. Psalms 51:17.

is the organ of the Shechinah, so *is the man whose love for God is perfect; "he becomes a living expression of God."*[40]

In the Messianic times the Holy Land will be called "the land of God's pleasure."[41] God will enter into a spiritual marriage with this land, and it will be transformed into paradise, the land of beauty and fertility. The sacramental nature of this union will be fully revealed. But even now this is, in a measure, true of those men who have become temples of the divine love; *they* are the land of God's pleasure. They experience the "divine soul" which is in them to work out His purpose. But as the grain must first die in the ground if it is to bring forth fruit, so must the subliminal divine soul enter entirely into man's nature and permit itself to be contained by it.

In the Messianic times God will remove the disease of self-satisfaction and self-righteousness from humanity and will accomplish what seems to us impossible.

Man, as he now is, is an incomplete being; the more he opens his heart to the divine influences, *"the more he grows into the image of the ideal man laid up in heaven."*[42]

Some writers base the expectation that the Messiah will reach a far higher state of perfection than man can ever reach, on Isaiah 52:13: "He shall be exalted and lifted up and *very high.*" In His time everything in nature, even evil itself, will be absorbed in

---

[40]   See *Shnei HaMeorot* 9*; cf. Odes of Solomon 26:10.

[41]   Isaiah 62:4 (*hephtzi bah*, [חפצי בה]) ["My delight is in her"].

[42]   *Adam Kadmon* [אדם קדמון] in Kabbalistic literature; cf. the *Nasha Kadmaia* of the Manichaeans, and the *Gabra Kadmaia* of the Mandaeans; not to be confused with *Adam HaRishon* [אדם הראשון] (the first man in opposition to all later men); cf. 1 Corinthians 15:49 and Philo, *Allegorical Interpretations* 1:31ff. Both St. Paul and Philo must have known an old tradition; cf. Richard Reitzenstein, *Poimandres: Studien zur griechisch-ägyptischen und frühchristlichen Literatur* (Leipzig: Teubner, 1904), 81; Wilhelm Bousset, *Die Religion des Judentums im späthellenistischen Zeitalter* (Berlin: Reuther & Reichard, 1903), 405; Johannes Weiss, *Der erste Korintherbrief* (Göttingen: Vandenhoeck und Ruprecht, 1910), 375.

Adam [אדם] stands for Adam [א], David [ד], *Mashiach* [מ], the ideal man and his historical prototypes; cf. *Sha'arei HaTeshuvah* 17*; *Torah Or* 15, 96* and often.

God, and the heathen, attracted by the fullness of His love, will give themselves up to Him voluntarily.

The partial rest which the pious experience now is often contrasted with that "Sabbath of the soul" in the Messianic times which God is preparing for those who love Him. Even in God Himself two kinds of rest are distinguished. He rested on the first Sabbath of creation, and yet He still goes on working, preparing creation for the appearance of His kingdom in the Messianic times. The aim of the divine architect will be reached when the building of His kingdom will be finished. But the perfect Sabbath of God will only begin when He actually *settles* in His kingdom in order to rule.[43] It is likened unto a man who builds a house for himself. While the house is being built he rests occasionally in order to gather strength to go on afterwards with the work; when the house is finished he rests from his *labors.* Only when he finally *settles* in the house *to live in it, he rests,* in the full sense.

And as to humanity in general, the world is made for *man,* but when he becomes a slave of this world and separates himself from God, he does harm not only to his own nature but to the whole creation.[44]

The essence of sin consists, therefore, in man's self-sufficiency before God. Man is endowed by God with a measure of the divine creative power. This endowment demonstrates both the love of God, and also man's divine origin, but if man does not recognize his dependence on God and instead chooses to isolate himself from God he soon becomes a worshipper of himself. "The whole creation groans" [45] because of this perversion

---

[43] That is in the post-Messianic time. Hosea 6:2, "On the third day He will revive us and we will live before Him," is used eschatologically for the perfect rest in the post-Messianic Age. *Torah Or*, Genesis, 8c–9c. Cf. with this Hebrews 4:1–11.

[44] On this old Jewish idea, of creation being subject to vanity and the renovation of nature in the Messianic times, cf. W. Sanday and Arthur C. Headlam, *International Critical Commentary to the New Testament: A Critical and Exegetical Commentary on the Epistle to the Romans* (New York: Scribner, 1896), 205–206, 209, on Romans 8:18, 23.

[45] [Romans 8:22.]

of man, for he comes to think not only of himself but also of the universe as something which it is possible to separate from God, the Creator of all. Everything is longing for the Messianic redemption, through which God's immanence will be fully realized. "The lower water weeps: 'I want to be with the King.'" [46]

We must enter deeply into this groaning of creation and listen with the ears of the Spirit to the plaint of the imprisoned soul of nature and its longing for redemption.

When all our thoughts and actions are the outcome of divine inspiration, then we unite everything that is seemingly separated from and independent of God with Him. And so we cooperate with Him in His redemptive activities and prepare the way for the Messiah. The following parable illustrates this:

A king lost a costly pearl. He sent out his three sons to find it. The first set out, glad to be free from the restraint of his father's presence. He cared neither for the pearl nor for his father. He never returned, but spent his life in following his own pleasure. The second set forth, made a hasty search, and quickly returned to his father's house, not because he so greatly loved his father but because he was loath to be away so long from the comforts of his home. Now, the third set out, full of sorrow at leaving his home and his beloved father, but determined, *notwithstanding all his own suffering and separation, to stay away and make diligent*

---

[46] *Torah Or* 11*; *Likkutei Torah,* Deuteronomy, 21ff.* Cf. *Genesis Rabbah* 5:3, "The waters under the earth," referred to in Genesis 1, stand for the material, and "the waters above the earth" for the spiritual world. The idea underlying this symbolic interpretation is evidently suggested by the difference between the tangible heaviness of the ocean and the aerial lightness of the clouds, and perhaps also the fact of tides governing the seas, while clouds float hither and thither at the whim of the wind. Ezekiel 47:12 is often used to bring out the idea of the cosmic redemption in the future eon. It is very probable that John 7:37–38 refers to the same passage and that instead of εκ της κοιλιας ["from the innermost being," *ek tes koilias*] we have to read εκ του θρονου ["from the throne," *ek tou thronou*] (the Aramaic *kursayeh* [כורסיה], "his throne," instead of *karseh* [כרסה], "his belly"). Cf. Rendel Harris, "Rivers of Living Waters," *The Expositor* 8th series: 20 (1920): 197–202.

search until he should find the pearl, because he knew what great joy the finding of it would give to his father.

One man is altogether absorbed in the things of this world. Another is eager to please God, not out of love for Him, but because he is afraid to lose the future bliss in paradise. But there are some men who love God for His own sake and search for the *divine sparks*[47] which are scattered in this world, in man and nature, and try to bring them back to their source.[48]

Man has been created by God in order that he may finish what God has deliberately left unfinished. Not that God needs the help of His creatures, but it is His love which causes Him to impart His own Nature to the work of His hands, in order that man should have the privilege and joy of becoming His fellow-worker in this world, in natural as well as in spiritual life.

Moreover, in a certain sense God *does* need men, in order to exercise His kingship. A king needs a people that accept his rule *voluntarily.* God, by virtue of His character, needs a being to whom He can reveal Himself, whom He can love, and through whom He can shed abroad His light and life.[49]

The ultimate issues of this truth are of the most vital and cosmic significance, *for God Himself is affected by our life.* When a mother suckles her child, the amount of her milk is increased in proportion to the vigor with which the child sucks. In like manner, the reservoirs of God are increased the more we draw from them for holiness, grace, and love.[50] On the other hand, "if Israel neglects the will of God, the higher Powers wax feeble."[51] There is a reciprocal giving and receiving.

We must try our best to become vessels for God's love, guard our hearts wherein dwells the "divine spark" and preserve it

---

[47] The "divine sparks," *nitzotzot* [ניצוצות], play the same role in the Jewish mystical terminology as in Plotinus. Cf. Tatian, *Address to the Greeks* 13; Tertullian, *A Treatise on the Soul* 41.

[48] *Ketonet Pasim,* 8*; cf. *Sha'arei HaTefillah* 60–66*.

[49] *Pirkei DeRabbi Eliezer* 3; *Exodus Rabbah* 23:1.

[50] *Shomer Emunim,* 55*.

[51] An old Jewish conception, cf. *Sifre* on Deuteronomy, 346.

undimmed and entire, and flee from "Egypt" in order to experience God's revelation on "Sinai." We must first try to clear away the thorns and weeds—hatred, jealousy, and lust—from the vineyard of the soul, so that that which is good in us may be separated from that which is evil. Then only can He fill us with His love. When God is sanctified by Israel, then He fulfills His promise: "I the Lord will sanctify you."

The following parable describes the divine love which is revealed in the mystery of the human personality, in "the descent of the soul, in order to inhabit a material tabernacle:"[52]

A king had an only son who was pure, wise, and good, having never known evil. The father delighted in these qualities of his son, and the son gloried in the wisdom of his father, and the harmony between them was perfect. One day, the wise king called his son to him and commanded him to prepare himself for a long journey into a far country. The son was loath to leave his father, but never doubting the wisdom of the command, he obeyed it. Often, as he wandered far from his father's home, he was sad and lonely. Horrible sights and sounds made him shudder. Temptations assailed him on all sides. What a struggle was his to keep himself unspotted. In this way, every day, unconsciously, he grew in strength of character. Meanwhile, the father longed unceasingly for the return of his son. His heart ached for the wanderer and suffered silently with him in each suffering. But how he rejoiced, even more than the son, at the latter's victory over temptation.[53]

---

[52] Cf. *Likkutei Torah*, Numbers, 20a ff. and often; *Zohar* III, 93a*. The doctrine of the pre-existence of the soul, which is fully developed in the Kabbalah, is also to be found in 2 Enoch 23:4 [longer recension], and *Wisdom of Solomon* 8:19–20. It is also suggested in 4 Ezra 4:33–43 and often. Cf. Frank Chamberlin Porter, "The Pre-existence of the Soul in the Book of Wisdom and in the Rabbinical Writings," *Old Testament and Semitic Studies* 1(1908): 205–270.

[53] Rabbi Dov Ber, *Sha'ar HaTefillah* 3*; *Torah Or*, Genesis, 8ff., 21ff.* Song of Songs 3:10, "The midst thereof is paved *with love*," refers, according to *Zohar* (I, 44c*; II, 97a; II, 127a), to the innermost palace of heaven, where stands the throne of God. This is often quoted in our sources to emphasize the truth that love is not merely an *attribute* of God, but His very nature.

2

THE LAW AND LOVE

To the Chasid, Scripture is full of spiritual truth, and even the Hebrew letters of the book are considered to be "vehicles which bring to the upper and lower worlds life from the divine centre." [54] He who comprehends the spiritual meaning of the Word of God and receives it into the innermost chambers of his heart is called "the friend and brother of God, and the holy temple of the divine Spirit." [55]

The deepest longing, therefore, of the genuine Chasid is to become a "living Torah." The keeping of the Law is to him only a means to an end: union with God. And for this reason he tries to keep the Law scrupulously, for "God's thoughts are embodied in it." Although at the present age not even the most saintly man fully understands the hidden spiritual meaning of the commandments, yet they must be "sown in tears";[56] i.e., observed without questioning. The "reaping in joy" [57] will be realized in the Messianic Age. For great will be the joy when the divine mysteries hidden in the Law will be fully unfolded by *Him* to whom Isaiah 52:13 ("Behold my servant will deal wisely") is applied.[58]

However, it is possible *"to keep all the commandments, and yet be far from God."* To such a man the Law can become, to use

---

[54] *Likkutei Torah* 50ff.* and often.

[55] *Likkutei Torah* 36*.

[56] [Psalms 126:5.]

[57] [Psalms 126:6.]

[58] *Likkutei Torah* 33*; cf. *Zohar* III, 260b*.

a Pauline phrase, "a savor of death unto death."[59] The Chasidic writers similarly use the old talmudic term *sam mavet* ("a deadly poison," [סם מות]). This poison can be cured only by the "salt" of the spirit of God, as Elisha cured the poisonous water with salt (2 Kings 2:19–22).[60]

Isaiah 66:1 ("The heaven is my throne and the earth my foot-stool") is often allegorically interpreted to describe the union of the heavenly with the earthly, the spiritual with the material, the infinite with the finite, in the Torah. The Torah is the "descending of the divine wisdom from the highest heights and embodying itself in 'earthly' commandments."[61] In these commandments God reveals His will and wisdom, which are really one with Him. Thus, it is not an exaggeration to speak of this conception of the Law as the Jewish doctrine of the "real Presence." Technically it is expressed in the words *"The LORD is in the wisdom"* (Wisdom = Torah).[62]

The cloud which surrounded Moses emanated from God. It sustained him during the forty days and nights when he "ate no bread, nor drank any water." It symbolizes the Law. It also emanates from God Himself and becomes Israel's spiritual food, and if they duly receive it, God's will embodies itself in their thoughts, words, and deeds.[63] For the fire of God's holy love needs "fuel" in order to burn. Israel is symbolized by the seven-branched candle-stick in the Tabernacle, the menorah, for through the possession of the Law they are destined to be "divine light-carriers."[64]

But, although the Torah is the revelation of God's will, yet *His innermost secret is known only to His most intimate friends,*

---

[59] [2 Corinthians 2:16.]

[60] *Likkutei Torah* 10*; *Torah Or* 71ff.*; cf. also Mark 9:50.

[61] Cf. *Torah Or*, Genesis, 13b–13d.

[62] Cf. Proverbs 3:19 [which can be literally read to say, "The LORD is in Wisdom." The "Wisdom" in Proverbs 3:19 is symbolically understood to refer to the Torah. Thus the sense is that the LORD is in the Torah.]

[63] *Likkutei Torah* 38*; [*Torah Or*, Genesis, 16a–b].

[64] *Likkutei Torah*, Numbers, 28a ff.

who, through their perfect fellowship with Him, are the only true representatives of Israel.[65]

The idea that a "more excellent way"[66] than legalism exists is not unknown to Jewish traditional piety. This can be specially seen from the following characterization, in some Chasidic writings, of different types of saintliness:

Some souls, it is said, are like birds. Their movements are graceful, their flight easy, in the rare atmosphere above earthly things. They are not bound by laws that govern those who must plod below.

Others are like those angels, representatives of the cosmic forces, whom Ezekiel symbolizes as having the faces of oxen and lions. That is to say, those souls are naturally heavy, dull, or fierce, but by their close contact with God are enabled to overcome their original nature and gain the power of flight, but not in so easy and natural a manner as the first. So, *to some few men because of their whole-hearted love for God, it becomes natural to live in harmony with the divine will, independent of the Law.*

The majority of Israel can only attain this high spiritual experience by unceasing effort and unquestioning obedience to the Law.[67]

The law of love is derived from the love of God. The more we love Him, the better we will love men.[68] We must look at man with the eyes of God and love him as God loves him.[69]

Love is not the same as natural kindliness. "Israel is by nature merciful," but love means something more: conquering our natu-

---

[65] *Torah Or 50*.

[66] [1 Corinthians 12:31.]

[67] *Likkutei Torah* 36–38*; *Torah Or,* Genesis, 16a–b; cf. *Zohar* I, 122a; II, 166b, 217b.

[68] See *Tanya* 32 and for parallels in early rabbinic, cf. my *Die religiöse Denkweise der Chassidim*, 89.

[69] For the combination of love for God and love for man, cf. *Testament of Twelve Patriarchs, Testament of Issachar* 5; *Testament of Dan* 5. For rabbinic parallels, see Abrahams, *Studies in Pharisaism and the Gospels: First Series* (Cambridge: Cambridge University Press, 1917), 18–29.

ral tendencies and sacrificing our own wills on God's altar, loving even him who is unlovable, having mercy upon those who seem to us to be unworthy, *bringing down the grace of God to sinners and to Gentiles,*[70] condescending to the lowest, the most degraded, because of the good that is hidden in them, because of the "divine spark" which is dormant even in the greatest sinner.[71]

Israel is the *"measure of the Godhead"*[72] and every individual Israelite is a part of this measure. In one sense, the head is of greater importance than the feet in a body, yet the feet have the advantage over the head because they carry the whole body, the head included.

So must we love not only the learned and the pious, but also the ignorant and the unspiritual, in order that the body may be whole and active.

The essence of love is love for the divine essence in man. As the lightning breaks through the clouds, so does the hidden light of God break through the material veil of this world when there is love in us. As the sun scatters the darkness, so should our love lighten dark and sad hearts. Our relation to all men should be one of friendship. But there are two kinds of friendship. There are friends who can bring the greatest sacrifices for one another but who are all the time conscious of it. Others are like David and Jonathan; they become almost one soul, and each rejoices in having to suffer for the sake of the other.

Love for man is more to God than the outward keeping of the whole Law. Through love even our body becomes an organ of the Shechinah, and we become united with the spiritual world and are able, through our prayers, to bring down grace out of the heart of God.[73] Our love should not be measured; it should have no limit.

---

70 Cf. *Tomer Devorah* 3; *Likkutei Ramal* 9*.

71 For the idea of the *imitatio Dei* [Latin: "imitation of God"] in Pharisaic literature cf. Solomon Schechter, *Some Aspects of Rabbinic Theology* (New York: Macmillan, 1909), 199–218. See also *The Letter of Aristeas* 188, 210, 281; cf. b.*Sotah* 14a.

72 See *Tomer Devorah* 2; *Likkutei Torah,* Deuteronomy, 71c ff.

73 Often; cf. Siddur (*Sha'arei HaTefillah*)*; *Tanya* 4, 23.

Only the perfect man must limit his love, in order that the *evil powers should not misuse the abundance of his goodness.*[74]

We should not reward evil with evil, *but forgive our enemies and try to bring them to God.* When we love our heavenly Friend we cannot endure that men should blaspheme Him and live without Him. As a father rejoices when his children are loved by others, so our heavenly Father rejoices when we love even His prodigal sons and try to bring them back to the "wings of the Shechinah." He rejoices when we long for the time of the Messiah, when there will be no more evil and when "they will bring forth no corruption upon His holy mountain."[75]

That the Messianic Age will bring not merely a revelation of the hidden meaning of the *old* Law, but a *new* revelation, has been shown above.[76]

The following differentiation between the Mosaic and the Messianic revelations can be considered as a summary of Jewish mystic thought on the subject:

The Law was given through Moses in order to bring forth a union between God and Israel, as between bridegroom and bride, but not as between husband and wife. In the Messianic Age the perfect union will be established. The Sinaitic revelation manifested only "the outer side of the divine will"; in the days of the Messiah the inner nature of God will be revealed, and His light

---

[74] Ibid.

[75] [Isaiah 65:25.] Cf. *Tomer Devorah* 2–4; *Likkutei Ramal* 9*; *Zohar* II, 69b–70a; *Likkutei Torah*, Deuteronomy, 48*. *Likkutei Torah*, Numbers, 101*; *Torah Or*, Exodus, 92, 101*.

[76] See also [*Song of Songs Rabbah* 1:2]: Rabbi Yehudah said: "When the Israelites heard the words 'I am the Lord Thy God' (Exodus 20:2), they were meant to study the Torah in such a way that they should never forget it. They asked Moses to teach them. But soon they forgot it all. Said they: 'Who is Moses? He is only a man (flesh and blood); as *he*, so will his *Torah* cease to be!' They turned to him again, and said: 'Moses, our master! Oh, if God would only reveal Himself again to us! Oh, if He were to kiss us with the kisses of *His* mouth! Oh, if only His Torah were to enter into our innermost hearts!' Moses answered: 'In this dispensation it cannot be, but it will take place in the coming dispensation (Messianic Age).'" Jeremiah 31:33 (the new covenant) is quoted.

will permeate man.[77] It is very characteristic that this Messianic revelation is described[78] as *chesed dikshot* ("the grace of truth," [חסד דקשוט]).

---

[77] Cf. *Torah Or,* 92*.

[78] *Likkutei Torah,* Numbers, 101*.

3

FEAR AND LOVE

P hilo[79] and the rabbis[80] often discuss the relationship between fear of God and love of God. In our Chasidic sources we find the following differentiations:

In the deepest recesses of our hearts fear and love dwell together; they reveal themselves in joy. We rejoice in the consciousness of God's love and nearness but tremble at the same time because of the awfulness of His presence. This is the Chasidic interpretation of Psalms 2:11: "Be glad with trembling." [81] Abraham and Isaac symbolize love and fear respectively.[82] But both Abraham (representing love of God) and Isaac (representing fear of God) can have their abode in the same human breast.

To the Chasid everything that has even an appearance of evil becomes a thick wall of partition between him and God,[83] and his soul is consequently full of fear and trembling before Him. Such a fear is considered to be an original endowment of every

---

[79] For instance *The Special Laws* 1:300; cf. also *Wisdom of Ben Sira* 1:11ff., 2:15–16, 10:19, 25:11.

[80] Cf. the discussion between Joshua ben Hyrkanos and Joshua ben Hanania in m.*Sotah* 5:5.

[81] *Likkutei Torah*, Deuteronomy, 45a. Cf. *Seder Eliyahu Rabbah* 3; *Chovot Halevavot, The Gate of the Love of God* 1.

[82] "Abraham, my *beloved*" (Isaiah 41:8). ("Beloved" in Ephesians 1:6 is probably also based on the same verse. The Messiah, the seed of Abraham, being *the* beloved.) "The *Fear* of Isaac" (Genesis 31:42).

[83] "Flee from every evil and from whatsoever is similar to it" (*Didache* 3:1), is the very essence of traditional Jewish piety; cf. t.*Chullin* 2:24.

Israelite. But the highest form of fear is the one which is the result from true knowledge of God's love for man and nature. The greatest sinner, if he would but reflect on how God's glory fills and overshadows the "upper and lower worlds," would pause in fear before he sins. There is a difference, however, between fear of *sin*, which is due to the consciousness of God's sublime holiness, and the fear of *God*, which is the result of an intense realization of His immanence in the universe. "Fear ye before the Lord" (Psalms 33:8) denotes the fear of God as He is manifested in creation and in natural forces, while "Fear ye the Lord" (Psalms 34:9) means the fear of the awful and transcendent God, the divine law-giver. The realization of God's holiness only intensifies the sense of our absolute remoteness from Him: God and man remain separate. But the realization that He is omnipresent generates a fear which leads to the experience that God is all and man is nothing.

Only in the days of the Messiah will everyone experience such a fear.

When the King comes, some men are filled with a guilty fear and flee from his presence. But the King's friends rejoice. So there is a fear of God which causes men to flee from Him and one which causes them to dance before Him with joy. "The sea saw it and fled; the mountains danced like lambs" (Psalms 114:3–4) is the allegorical expression of this thought.[84]

Our love for God must be pure, untainted by hope of reward or fear of punishment. "He does not truly love the King, who looks to him for some favor."[85]

We should love Him above all things and suffer sorrow gladly for His sake. Our love for God should not be less than our duty towards our fellow men. We are obliged to strengthen the weak in order that the whole body may benefit, "*so we must strengthen the*

---

[84] *Sha'ar HaTefillah* 22ff.*; *Likkutei Torah,* Numbers, 5*; cf. *Exodus Rabbah* 21:6.

[85] *Tanya* often; cf. m.*Avot* 1:3.

Shechinah,[86] which is sick from love"[87] and which "for our sakes has borne our griefs and carried our sorrows."[88]

As it is our duty to be hospitable to wayfarers and to receive them as our guests, so *should we receive God into our hearts*. As the Jews honor the dead by washing their bodies and clothing them in white garments, so should they wash off the spots with which their sins have stained the Shechinah, "and help Her to ascend from the depths into the heights."

As it is the duty to help to bring about pure marriages among the people, so should we, through our true love for God, further "the union of the divine bridegroom with His bride Israel."[89]

This love for God brings forth a union with Him and with the spiritual universe which the human mind cannot grasp nor the tongue describe.

Fear and love are wings by which the soul is carried to heaven. As it is with fear, so it is with love. There is a natural inborn love of the soul for its native home as the flame by nature leaps upward, and there is an *"amor Dei intellectualis"* [Latin: "intellectual love of God"].[90] The inborn love always ascends to heaven. As the flame by its nature always strives to separate itself from the wick in order to enter into its own more aerial element, so does the soul, by its very nature, seek to unite itself with its source. No child really knows the true nature of his father and why he should love him, yet the soul of the child is closely united with the soul of his father. Just as all the riches of the world are as nothing in comparison with the love that we have for our own life, *so the*

---

86 In traditional Jewish theology the Shechinah denotes the diffused Divine Presence in creation, and more especially in His dealings with His people in their dispersion.

87 Cf. Song of Songs 5:8.

88 Isaiah 53 is often applied to the suffering Shechinah.

89 *Tomer Devorah* 5.

90 This term has been taken over by Spinoza from Jewish oral tradition. [Baruch (Benedict) de Spinoza (1632–1677) was a famous Dutch philosopher of Jewish descent.]

accumulation of good works, through the keeping of the Law, is nothing in comparison with this natural love of the soul for God.[91]

The fellowship with God which comes from such a love is so all-pervading, and leads to a self-surrender so complete, that the result is joy ineffable. Such love cannot, at times, endure the limitations of the body; the heart cannot contain it.

Numbers 8:1–4 is interpreted as follows:

The divine pattern of the menorah is Israel (as it exists in the idea of God). God desires that the flame of their love should ascend to heaven. The mediators of this love, the seven lamps, are "the seven shepherds,"[92] the heavenly representatives of Israel, the greatest of whom is the prototype of the High Priest Aaron. For Moses and Aaron are "the friends of God—the Bridegroom, and of Israel—His bride." Moses, the friend of the Bridegroom, brings the infinite Light of God to Israel; and Aaron, the friend of the bride, leads Israel to her Bridegroom.[93]

In the heart of the sinner this love for God is in a state of slumber. But at some great crisis in his life this love may awaken, and then he begins to long not only for the bliss of God's paradise, but for God Himself.[94] Man is a microcosm, in whom are to be found the elements of the whole cosmos, even the characteristics of the manifold celestial beings. There are some men in whom the seraphic fire is always burning brightly. Like the seraphim, the substance of their song is nothing else but "Holy, holy, holy." But there are others in whom the fire glows faintly and whose spark must be blown into flame. As there is a love like fire, so there is a love like water. The mutual love of father and child is like a smooth-flowing river. The love of a bridegroom for his bride is like fire which rises and falls; it is impetuous. Our love for God

---

[91] See *Sha'arei HaTeshuvah* 22a* (on Song of Songs 8:7); cf. 1 Corinthians 13:3.

[92] Cf. "the seven pillars of the world" in the *Clementine Homilies* [18:13–14] and the allegorical interpretation of the "seven shepherds and the eight princes" (Micah 5:5) in [b.*Sukkah* 52b] and b.*Chagigah* 12b.

[93] *Likkutei Torah*, Numbers, 4*; *Torah Or*, Genesis, 53, 57*; cf. *Pirkei de Rabbi Eliezer* 41.

[94] See *Tanya* 19; *Likkutei Torah* 39, 172*; *Torah Or* 166*.

is sometimes smooth and continuous, and sometimes it bursts into flame, corresponding to our experience of God's love for us. For we are either struck by His *fatherly* love or by that love which comes down even to the abode of sin, in order to save sinners and turn darkness into light.[95]

This latter, *condescending* love of God is an act of His will, for it is supra-rational (humanly speaking), yet it is the highest wisdom of God. When we realize this aspect of God's love, our love for Him also becomes something impetuous, like fire. But such love is not born of the reason, but of the will. When our friend is in danger, we venture our life to save him; we do not weigh the sacrifice, we do not reason.

To him who has such a love for God "is given the name '*son of God*' and all power over the treasures and mysteries of God."[96] Such a love is the possession of a few elect souls who sacrifice themselves for God's sake, take on themselves the yoke of the Law joyously, are humble, gentle, and forgiving. All of this they do not only for their own sakes, but in order to "sanctify the Name of God (*kiddush HaShem*, [קדוש השם])," "to raise the Shechinah out of the dust."[97]

---

[95] Cf. *Torah Or*, Exodus, 124*; *Likkutei Torah*, Deuteronomy, 96*. Song of Songs 5:2 is often thus allegorized to express the relationship between God and Israel: "Hearken! My beloved knocks. Open to me, my sister—my friend." Israel is the *sister* of God; their mutual love is a natural one. But her heart is not always responsive; sin and self-righteousness, the desire to be something in herself, the love of the world, harden her heart. During prayer and the study of God's Word and in the keeping of His commandments we do realize, more or less, His sublime holiness and love, and are moved to love Him. But He desires that we should constantly feel this *sisterly* love for Him. He knocks at our heart and says, "Open!" When we make an opening in our hearts, "if only as small as the eye of a needle," then God increases it so that it becomes "as wide as the Temple."

[96] See *Shnei HaMeorot* 24*; *Shomer Emunim* 16*.

[97] See above page 51. Sin affects God; cf. b.*Megillah* 29a; y.*Ta'anit* 1:1; [*Exodus Rabbah* 23:5]; *Zohar* II, 7a, 9a–9b and often; *Torah Or*, Exodus, 125*; *Likkutei Torah* on Deuteronomy, 64, 85*.

4

JOY AND LOVE

J oy is the keynote of Chasidic piety. The Pauline "rejoice, and again I say unto you rejoice"[98] has a genuine Chasidic sound. In some of the documents it is very subtly differentiated between the joy which is experienced on special occasions, for instance during prayer, and the joy which is always potentially present. The one increases the other. When we rejoice at the nearness of God, this hidden divine joy so fills our whole personality that it shines through us and we become transfigured. "Wine that maketh glad the heart of man and oil to make his face to shine"[99] is interpreted in this sense.[100]

The joy which results from the study of God's Word and from keeping the commandments does not reveal itself equally at all times. Of all the feasts, that of Tabernacles is the most joyous. For this reason, water, and not wine, was used in the oblation at the Temple services on this festival; the joy, which the wine symbolized ordinarily being actually experienced.[101]

The vine is a symbol of Israel, the grapes being individual Israelites. As the wine is hidden in the grapes, so is the joy of the love of God hidden in the soul.

---

[98] [Philippians 4:4.]

[99] Psalms 104:15.

[100] Cf. *Torah Or* 96*: "Wine gladdens"; i.e., the joy experienced during prayer; oil "makes the face (the whole personality) shine; i.e., the potential joy."

[101] Cf. *Likkutei Torah*, Deuteronomy 17c ff. and 79d ff.

However, as the grapes must be trodden and the skins left behind in the winepress in order that the good wine should gush forth, so does pure, joyous love towards God pour forth from our hearts only when it is trodden out humbly in God's winepress and the skin of our self-righteousness left behind.[102] Self-righteousness is idolatry and prolongs the exile of Israel and of the Shechinah.[103]

It is supposed that the best wine comes from grapes which are nearest the soil; so real joy in God is said to be found only where there is humility. This humility is a gift of God. Without the awakening and inspiration from above, we see neither God nor ourselves in the true light. The only thing we can do without His aid is to fight against Him. Moses was great because he was humble. He said of himself, "And we, what are we?" (Exodus 16:7). His soul also came *"from the light of the Father Himself."*[104]

In our relationship to God we should be like servants who walk *behind* and follow their master, in order that we may be found worthy to reach the state of disciples, who walk *with* their master, later on. "Follow *behind* your Lord" (Deuteronomy 13:5). When we know how far we are from God, just then He is near us. But when we think that we are near Him, then He is afar off, "From the *distance* God appeared to me" (Jeremiah 31:3). *There is more hope for the greatest sinner than for the righteous who knows not his sinfulness.*[105]

"God can only dwell in broken vessels." This is a frequently used phrase.

The aim of all Creation is *bittul hayesh* ["abnegation of being," בטול היש]; that is, ceasing from being something apart from God; *to die, in order to be raised to life again.* Every world fulfills its

---

[102] Cf. *Exodus Rabbah* 26:1ff. Israel is like an olive. Just as this fruit yields its precious oil only after being much pressed and squeezed, so Israel's testing is one of great oppression, in order that it may thereby give forth its illuminating wisdom.

[103] Often in Talmud and Midrash. Cf. b.*Sotah* 5a; b.*Eruvin* 13b. See *Zohar* I, 120b; *Likkutei Torah* 5, 26, 30*.

[104] Cf. *Torah Or* 95*.

[105] *Likkutei Torah*, Deuteronomy, 130*.

mission of dying to itself according it its own degree and in its own way.[106]

The keeping of the Law does not profit us unless it is done joyfully. "We must believe in the light of the countenance of the living King." He is perfectly good. "Let us therefore rejoice in Him always."[107]

If we have no joy in our hearts, we deny the love of God.[108] We should not say, "Our heart is a dwelling place of lust, jealousy, anger; there is no hope for us." Let us realize that we have another guest in us who desires to give us life and joy, notwithstanding our sin. Even if we are disturbed by worldly thoughts during our most intimate converse with God, we should not lose courage and joy. "It only proves the reality of our fellowship with God, if Satan tries to disturb it."[109]

This joy is the revelation of the inner life of God in us. It is not what the world calls joy. As the air enters into the body of a bird and enables it to fly, so does the joy of God come from the spiritual world and fills the heart, enabling it to lift itself up above time and space. When the soul is in its highest flight, then it sees without eyes, listens without ears, speaks without language, and its song, when it ascends to rejoice "at the body of the King," is a song without words.[110]

There is a subtle difference between joy and delight. We *rejoice* over some precious possession, even though it may not be con-

---

[106] *Likkutei Torah*, Deuteronomy, 87*, on humility. Cf. 1 Enoch 108; 2 Enoch 25; *Testament of the Twelve Patriarchs, Testament of Reuben* 3; *Testament of Gad* 5; *Testament of Joseph* 10; *Testament of Benjamin* 5; *Letter of Aristeas* 262ff., 269; 4 Ezra 8:49ff.; *Prayer of Azariah* 16, 65, and Hillel's utterance: "My humiliation is my exaltation and my exaltation is my humiliation" (*Leviticus Rabbah* 1:5).

[107] Often, see *Likkutei Torah* 73*.

[108] *Igeret HaKodesh* 11.

[109] Cf. *Likkutei Torah*, Deuteronomy, 85, 94*; *Likkutei Torah*, Leviticus, 35*. Cf. *Tanya* 28 and *The Shepherd of Hermas* on joy and sadness [e.g., 1:1, 2:2].

[110] See *Likkutei Torah*, Leviticus, 96*. Cf. *Chovot Halevavot, The Gate of Self-Accounting* 3.

tinually before our eyes—as, for instance, in a hidden treasure. When we visit the secret hiding place of our treasure, uncover it, and see it dazzling before our eyes, then we *delight* in it. The Law is our treasure, in which we rejoice. It is a *hidden* treasure because the deepest spiritual meaning is as yet not made perfectly clear to us. Yet one thing we know: it is the revelation of God, and this makes it very precious to us. But the day will come when the divine mysteries of the Law will be unfolded by the Messiah, and we shall see God face to face. Then our souls will be filled with *delight*.[111]

---

[111] Cf. *Torah Or*, Genesis, 13b–13d.

5

PRAYER AND LOVE

That prayer should take a central position in Chasidic piety is only what is to be expected. The old traditional definition of prayer as *avodat halev* ("the service of the heart," [עבודת הלב]) is often used in Chasidic writings to emphasize the true character of worship. *Tefillah belo kavanah keguf belo neshamah* ("Prayer without intention is like a body without a soul," [תפילה בלא כונה כגוף בלא נשמה]). *Kavanah* ("intention," [כונה]) and *hitlahavut* ("enthusiasm, ecstasy," [התלהבות]) are the chief characteristics of true prayer. It means the concentration of the whole mind on God. The ideal prayer is not asking God for this or for that, but the desire that He may, so to speak, concentrate His whole mind upon us.

A king made a proclamation. He invited his subjects to come and lay before him the greatest desires of their hearts. They came in great numbers. Some asked for wealth, others for honors, some for wisdom, others for health and beauty. But one man came who, though he looked poor and wretched, asked for none of these things. What he desired was to have the privilege of seeing the king each day and of speaking to him personally, knowing that should the king grant him this request, all the other things would be his as well.

If we concentrate all our mental and spiritual faculties on Him, He will come down and concentrate His infinite creative power and love on us.[112]

In a candle flame there are two parts: the outward yellow flame and the inner blue one. So it is with the flame of the divine fire in our hearts. The outer flame is kindled by our understanding; namely, when we realize the sublimeness of God. When we meditate on His majesty and power, then a love is begotten in us which is "powerful as death, whose flames are flames of fire."[113] But the inner flame is at the center and depth of our heart. The love burning there is of a higher quality than that love which arises only from the knowledge of God's power. For just as we are often moved strongly by something that touches the innermost center of the heart, and we act and speak without reflection, so it is in our deepest communion with God at prayer. The fellowship with God resulting from our intellectual apprehension of Him is not as intense, by itself, as the worship of God which has its source in the depths of our personality, when it is illuminated not by our own wisdom but by the supreme *divine wisdom* which is above human understanding and knowledge. In this divine wisdom *the life of God Himself is enwrapped and hidden.*[114]

From this life and light proceeds the divine "spark" which is hidden in every soul. Not all men succeed in rising to this close union with God at prayer, because this spark is *imprisoned* in them. "Yea, even the Shechinah herself is imprisoned in us, for the spark *is* the Shechinah in our souls."[115]

Only through true prayer can the wall of partition between man and God be removed; only then can He use it for the gather-

---

[112] Cf. *Kuntras HaHitpa'alut*, 25*.

[113] Song of Songs 8:6.

[114] Proverbs 3:19 is used as a technical term to express this "Logos" [λογος] idea: "God Himself [is] in [His] wisdom."

[115] The rather difficult passage in Psalms 27:8, "My heart said unto thee, 'Seek ye my face,' *paneh* [פנה]," is interpreted thus: We should seek God in our *innermost heart (penimiut* ["inner-being," פנימיות]), "deep calleth unto deep" [(Psalms 42:7) i.e., the depth of man's heart calls out to the depth of God's being]. Cf. *Igeret HaKodesh* 4.

ing of these "sparks." This, according to Chasidic explanation, is why Israel longs so ardently for the restoration of the sacrificial system in the days of the Messiah, for this divine "spark" is also imprisoned in animals and in all creation. The coming of the Messiah, and with it the restoration of sacrifices, will mean also the restoration of all things, the ascending of all beings, through the Redeemer—"the ideal Adam."[116] Every real prayer has something of this character of sacrifice and brings nearer the Messianic redemption. If Israel would only pray in the true spirit, the Messiah would reveal Himself in all His glory now.[117]

Ecclesiastes 3:21 ["Who knows whether the spirit of man goes upward and the spirit of the beast goes down into the earth?"] is interpreted as being a description of the antithesis between the "divine" and the "natural" soul in man, especially during prayer. The divine soul is longing to unite itself with its source as indeed, as we have seen, it is a part of God Himself. But the natural soul strives more and more to descend into its material surroundings. They cannot possibly be at one any more than fire and water. But sometimes they must come to close grips; for instance, at prayer. Then a struggle between them begins. The "divine" soul has such an intense desire after God that it would carry the whole man with itself into higher spheres and spiritualize all his natural affections.

Not every prayer, however, has this character of a struggle. Sometimes the spirit of man is drawn, without any struggle, towards God, as the light of the candle in the daytime ceases to have individuality or as the soul in paradise is at home with God. The ideal Sabbath worship, for instance, is of this kind, when the

---

[116] *Torah Or* 96*. Cf. Ephesians 1:10: "That in the dispensation of the fullness of time He might *gather together in one* all things in Christ." In this connection note that the Hebrew word *me'od* ["abundance," מאד] in Isaiah 52:13 is often used to describe the ideal humanity of the Messiah, the perfect Adam. First, because the Hebrew letters form the word Adam [אדם]; and secondly, because these letters are the initials of Adam [א], David [ד], *Mashiach* [מ].

[117] Often in Talmudic and medieval literature. But see especially Zalman, Siddur, section on Prayer*.

spirit rejoices in God, in the contemplation of His love in creation and redemption. On every Sabbath the edifice is completed *if we do the will of God*. On this day the inner life of the Israelite is hidden with God.

On the other hand, the seven weeks between Passover and Pentecost represent the struggle between the two souls. At Pentecost the struggle is over; the "natural" soul is defeated by the "divine." This feast, therefore, symbolizes the spiritualization of natural life. On Passover leaven is forbidden because it stands for pride.[118] But at Pentecost, leaven symbolizes the sublime spirit of God which penetrates even the natural life, and therefore it had to be used in sacrifices at that feast.[119]

We may be disturbed during our most fervent prayers by alien powers which cling to us just when our spirit is in its closest approach to God. For as the thief risks his life only when he expects abundant treasure, so are the evil powers most insistent just when the praying soul is about to share the riches of God. The evil in man gathers strength from the life of the spirit at prayer. In the struggle between a saintly man and a godless one, something of the impurity of the latter must needs cleave to the former because of their close contact during the struggle.

But after prayer, when the struggle has come to an end, the evil thoughts cannot derive any more nourishment from the divinely strengthened soul. They are separated and scattered. This is the mystical interpretation of Psalms 92:9: "For lo, Thine enemies, oh Lord, for lo, Thine enemies shall perish; all the workers of iniquity shall be scattered abroad."

---

[118] Cf. Philo, *Fragment on Exodus 23:18*.

[119] Pentecost is also in mystic Judaism the "Feast of the Spirit" just because it is supposed to be the "time of the giving of the Law." With the exception of the "Parable of the Leaven" [Matthew 13:33; Luke 13:20–21] in the Synoptics, and this Chasidic symbolic interpretation, "leaven," always symbolizes something bad in Jewish traditional literature. For a similar application of the metaphor of the leaven, cf. *Perek HaShalom* 1. See also Nachmanides' commentary on Leviticus 23:17.

This struggle during prayer is carried on only by (to use a modern psychological term) the "conscious" souls, one of which is called in Chasidism "the inner light in the vessel of limitation." But the Jew's personality is also endowed with that very life of God, which cannot be contained in any "vessel of limitation." *This life surrounds his personality as a radiance, only to be perceived by spiritual vision,* just as God's immanence permeates the world in a mysterious way. It is not concerned in the struggle of the "souls" during prayer; it cannot be approached by any alien power.[120]

---

[120] Cf. *Likkutei Torah,* Deuteronomy, 75*; *Torah Or* 35*.

6

REPENTANCE AND LOVE

The inner heart of man is overlaid by an unclean covering: the lust of this world. This covering is technically called "Babylon," or "the foreskin of the heart." Conversion in the Chasidic sense is therefore "circumcision of the heart."[121] Now, in circumcision there are two operations; after the circumcision proper comes the uncovering of the corona,[122] without which circumcision is not valid. First the thick skin is circumcised, and then the thinner skin is stripped away. Similarly it is true of the spiritual circumcision. There are gross and subtle sins. It is not enough to be free from the former; the foreskin of the heart is still overlaid by the skin of subtle sins, which are even more difficult to lay aside.[123]

The motive for repentance should not be fear of the pangs of hell, but "the sorrow for our own soul which has fallen from its highest state to the depths of sin, from God's palace to the lower places of impurity."[124]

Fasting, although an outward expression of repentance, is not one of its essentials; on the contrary, "we shall have to give

---

[121] *Igeret HaKodesh* 4.

[122] *Periah* [פריעה], cf. y.*Shabbat* 19:6; [b.*Shabbat* 137a–b].

[123] Deuteronomy 30:6 is therefore explained eschatologically: the Messiah will bring forth the circumcision of the heart. Then the inner center of the heart will be revealed, and the Shechinah—the inner life of Israel—will be forever freed from Her exile.

[124] *Likkutei Torah* on Deuteronomy 1:22*. Cf. *Zohar* I, 27b and II, 97a.

account of everything in this world that we might have enjoyed and did not."[125] Food should not only strengthen us for God's service, but, by concentrating our minds on the giver of all good gifts, we should spiritualize the material and gather the "soul sparks" which are contained in the food, and help them to ascend with our prayers to heaven. For as the soul of man after death awaits in paradise the reunion with its spiritualized body at the general resurrection in the Messianic times, so does the soul of food (that is, the divine word by which a particular food has been created) await the reunion with its body; namely, the material part of the food. Through our thanksgiving before and after meals, we cooperate with God in this process of spiritualization.[126]

When the Messiah comes, God will gather the scattered sparks again and unite them with Himself.[127] But we should prepare the way for Him by repenting daily and by helping others to repent.

---

[125] y.*Kiddushin* 4:12—Isaiah 58:7—is often interpreted in this sense: we should not deny ourselves things necessary for our own body. Cf. *Sha'arei HaTeshuvah*, 6*. *Tanya* 37; also *Tanya* 7. *Hegion HaNefesh*, by Rabbi Abraham ben Chiyah, chapter 15*.

[126] *Likkutei Torah*, Numbers, 29a ff. *Torah Or* , Exodus, 65d ff. [Also see *Torah Or*, Genesis, 26a–d.]

[127] Deuteronomy 30:4, "When He will scatter thee to the ends of the world He will gather thee from thence," is used in an eschatological sense for the gathering of "divine sparks." "The air is full of such sparks of the souls of sinners who cannot enter into their rest" (cf. b.*Shabbat* 152b).—A holy man once saw in a vision the spirits of sinners. They floated restlessly to and fro before him, filling the air with their lamentations. He inquired of them the cause of their woe. They described to him how they were continually being driven out of the "heavenly mansions" because they would not repent while on earth. "Have mercy on us," they said. "Free us from our sufferings by your prayers, that we may find rest." Indeed the true saint can raise such souls to heaven. They cleave to his prayers and are carried along with them to God. Satan is then afraid to come near them there to disturb them. Moreover, the soul of the true saint *descends at death into hell, in order that the souls of sinners should cleave to it and ascend.* (The traditional Jewish view of Gehenna is that of a state of punishment of purification, through which every soul must pass.) Cf. *Kav HaYashar* (Wilna ed.), 17*.

Isaiah 29:19 ["The meek shall obtain fresh joy in the LORD, and the poor among mankind shall exult in the Holy One of Israel"] is thus interpreted: "The meek ones" are those whose joy in God increases through the keeping of the Law. But the "poor ones" are the repentant sinners, the spiritual beggars; "they will delight in the Holy One of Israel." Because they have no spiritual riches, no accumulation of good works, they have only *one* desire, God Himself. And He becomes their only joy.

Although it is God who first moves man to repentance, yet in His love He considers the penitent as being responsible for his own conversion.

The sinner, in whose soul the light of the divine fire has been quenched, *is greater, when he repents, than the righteous who have no need for repentance.* He lifts himself up above time and space. Since he possesses nothing in himself that could awaken spiritual life, he throws himself entirely into the arms of God.[128]

When Moses was to bring down the "forgiving love" of God to Israel, he had to stand upon a rock to receive it (Exodus 33:21). This is symbolic of the hidden love of God because of the "sparks" which are hidden in the rock. When a sinner is converted, he brings down the *hidden* fire of the divine love. This "forgiving love" of God passes all understanding. It is more wonderful than the "reasonable love" of God to the righteous.[129]

The love of man to God which comes from the keeping of the Law is a love which proceeds from the "outer side" of the heart, but the love which the repentant sinner feels for God comes from within the heart.[130] The "sin-forgiving love" of God is said to come from the "will of all wills"; that is, from the innermost sphere of God's heart, which is above His will that is revealed in the Law.

---

[128] *Likkutei Torah*, Exodus, 52*; *Likkutei Torah*, Numbers, 28*. See *Zohar* I, 129b. Spinoza's words about the forgiving love of God in his *Tractatus Theologico-Politicus* (1670), 178, were literally taken from Rabbi Chasdai Crescas's *Or HaShem* (Ferrara: 1555); cf. 64a*.

[129] *Tanya* 7.

[130] [*Tanya* 50, cf. *Igeret HaTeshuvah* 9].

This "will of all wills" will be perfectly manifested in the Messianic times.[131]

Therefore, on the Day of Atonement the high priest entered the Holy of Holies in white garments. White, representing all the other colors in union, denotes, in Chasidic symbolism, the pure forgiveness of God which is independent of man's work. Again, the garments were made of linen, because the flax has *one* flower on *one* stalk.[132] When the high priest entered the holy of holies, the place where God dwells *alone*, in order to make atonement for the people, dressed in linen garments, he represented God's forgiveness as being something *unique* and independent of man's piety and his good works.[133]

True repentance consists in the longing that God should let His countenance shine upon us, that His relationship to us should be the relationship of one personality to another; that He should know us from the depths of His being, and that His forgiveness should come to us from the innermost part of His will—not like that of a man who throws a gift behind his back to his enemy, in whose face he cannot look.[134]

Just as the Messiah comes unexpectedly,[135] the awakening of the sinner towards repentance comes unexpectedly. It is above our understanding and knowledge; it is a gift from God which proceeds from "the light of the upper countenance."

The following parables with the "prodigal" *motif* will show that this type of Jewish piety presents in the highest sense, a *praeparatio evangelica* [Latin: "preparation for the gospel"]:

The son who is always at home with his father does not fully realize the intensity of the love he bears to his father because of the deep unconscious joy which this companionship gives him. When, however, the son has journeyed into a far country, the

---

[131] [*Igeret HaTeshuvah* 6, 8, cf. *Igeret HaKodesh* 10].

[132] Cf. [b.*Yoma* 71b.]

[133] See *Likkutei Torah* 55–57*. For the symbolism of the high priest's vestments, cf. Josephus, *Antiquities of the Jews* 3:151–187.

[134] *Likkutei Torah*, Leviticus, 52*.

[135] Cf. b.*Sanhedrin* 97a.

longing for his home and his father takes possession of him with such power that he becomes aware of the strength and depth of his love. So it is with the sinner who is repentant. His love for God reveals itself "in the distance."[136]

Moreover, it sometimes happens that even while the son is in his father's house the latter hides his face from him for a while. This is in order that when he again reveals himself to his son, the latter may realize afresh how much his father means to him. So does God hide His face from us for a while when we have broken His Law, in order to let the light of His countenance shine upon us the more strongly when we turn to Him again.[137]

A king had two sons. The one was obedient to his will, the other a rebel who left his father's house and wandered away. When the wanderer returned, *the father's delight over him was greater than the joy he had felt in the continuous presence of the son who had stayed at home.*[138]

---

[136] *Likkutei Torah*, Leviticus, 52, 83*. [Cf. *Likkutei Torah*, Deuteronomy, 71c ff.]

[137] *Likkutei Torah*, Leviticus, 83*.

[138] Rabbi Aaron Halevi, *Sha'arei HaYichud*, 8*. This parable is often used also in connection with the joy and delight of God in the Messianic times when sin itself will be redeemed. For Talmudic references, cf. Abrahams, *Studies in Pharisaism*, 139–149. With these two parables cf. *Torah Or* 46–48*: "When we hear a bird talk we are filled with wonder and delight at this extraordinary phenomenon. *So are the angels in heaven filled with delight over a sinner that repents*; for his speech is changed, and he begins to learn the language of angels. But even in heaven perfect joy will only come in the days of the Messiah, when the heathen too will turn to the only true God, and Satan will be conquered forever." Cf. b.*Berachot* 31a: "It is forbidden to man, that his mouth be filled with laughter in *this* world (dispensation), as it is written, '*Then* our mouths will be filled with laughter, and our tongue with singing.' When is that to be? At the time when 'they shall sing among the heathen, the Lord hath done great things for them' (i.e., in the Messianic times)."

SAINT PAUL'S HYMN OF LOVE

[1 CORINTHIANS 13]

1. Though I speak with the tongues of men and angels but have not love, I am become a sounding brass or a tinkling cymbal.

2. And though I have power of prophecy and know all secrets and all knowledge, and if I have all faith, so that I move all mountains, but have not love, I am nothing.

3. And if I give away all that I have, and if I sacrifice my body, so that I may[139] glory [rightly] but I have not love, I profit nothing.

4. Love is long-suffering, full of kindness is love, love envieth not, makes no display, is not puffed up, does not masquerade,

5. Seeketh not her own, is not easily provoked, does not bear malice,

6. Rejoiceth not in injustice, but rejoiceth in truth.

7. Beareth all things, believeth all things, hopeth all things, endureth all things.

---

[139] Cf. A. Harnack, "The Apostle Paul's Hymn of Love," *The Expositor* 8th series: 3 (1912): 385–408, 481–503.

8. Love never ceaseth—whether there be prophecies, they shall be done away, whether there be tongues, they shall cease, whether there shall be knowledge, it shall vanish away;

9. For we know in part, and we prophesy in part,

10. But when that which is perfect is come, then that which is in part shall be done away.

11. When I was a child, I spoke as a child, pondered as a child, thought as a child, when I became a man, I put away what is of the child.

12. For now we see by means of a glass, in a riddle, but then from face to face: now I know in part but then shall I know even as also I am known.

13. And now abideth faith, hope, love, these three; but the greatest of these is love.

EPILOGUE
LOVE IN THE FOURTH GOSPEL

The predominant and determining note of the life of the early church is κοινωνια ("fellowship," [*koinonia*]). It is the realization of the highest ideal of Chasidism—i.e., *achdut* ["unity," אחדות]. The word implies a closeness of union approaching to identity: "The multitude of the believers were of one heart and of one soul."[140] Love was the essential and characteristic keynote of the Messianic fellowship. The Messiah is the personification of divine love. He showed what real love is. Therefore, to imitate Him means to love as He did.[141] The imitation of Him is the imitation of God.[142] To live for Him is to live for God.[143] But Christ's love is not only an *example* for the fellowship, but is the power which awakens love in it. His love is powerful because it is *God's Love*: "Who shall separate us from *the love of Christ*? Neither death nor life … shall be able to separate us from *the love of God* which is in Christ Jesus our Lord."[144] Because of its divine character, this love is wonderful; "it passeth all understanding."[145] The visible

---

140 [Acts 4:32.]

141 Matthew 20:28; John 13:34; Romans 15:2ff.; Ephesians 5:2; 1 Corinthians 11:1.

142 Ephesians 4:32–52; cf. Philippians 2:4ff.; 1 Peter 2:21ff.; 1 John 4:17.

143 Romans 6:11.

144 Romans 8:35, 39.

145 Ephesians 3:19.

presentation of this love is the death of Christ;[146] "He died for all that they which live should not henceforth live unto themselves, but unto Him."[147] Therefore, coldness towards Him bars the door to God's presence.[148]

But the most "Chasidic" writing in the New Testament is probably "the Gospel according to St. John." The following is a brief summary of Love as it is presented there:

The love of God is concentrated in the Messiah, His Son, and only through Him He loves the world. This love of the Father for His Son manifests itself in *giving*: "He gives Him all things."[149] The world belongs to the Messiah (cf. Psalms 2:8); Israel, and in them humanity, are "His own."[150] But God's greatest gift to Him is not the world, but His Spirit, the *Ruach HaKodesh* [רוח הקדש]. This He gives Him beyond measure.[151] Through the Spirit the Father enables Him to participate in His creative and redemptive activities: "He shows Him all that He doeth."[152] The Father knows Him, and He knows the Father.[153] This intimacy between Father and Son is the basis and the central expression of the Father's love.

The Son is the organ of God's love, and the intensity of this love is shown in the gift: "So God loved the world that He gave His only begotten Son." The reason for the Father's love for the world is the world's danger of perishing from want of "light" and "life"; i.e., of true knowledge of and communion with Him.[154]

God's love for His Son brings forth a corresponding love of the Son for Him. It expresses itself in the glorification, or sanctifica-

---

[146] Romans 5:8. Συνιστησιν ["demonstrates," *sunistesin*].

[147] 2 Corinthians 5:15. Cf. Romans 4:7; Philippians 2:30.

[148] 1 Corinthians 16:22.

[149] John 3:35.

[150] John 1:11.

[151] John 3:34.

[152] John 5:20.

[153] John 10:15.

[154] Light and life, perfect knowledge of God and communion with Him, which, as we have seen, is expected of the Messianic Age, is given through the Messiah. The expectation is founded chiefly on Jeremiah 24:7. Cf. with this the Hebraic expression in 1 John 5:20.

tion, of God's Name by the Son. This highest motive of Jewish piety, *kiddush HaShem* ["sanctification of the Name," קדוש השם], is His supreme objective. When the Son summarizes the work that He has done on earth, He does not refer to any empirical success, such as the love and faith which He had awakened among men, but the service which He had rendered to God: "I have *glorified* Thee on earth" (John 17:4). He lives and dies for God's honor. His love is a conscious self-oblation to the will of God.[155]

His will is "to finish the work of Him who sent Him."[156] He must help men in their misery and need in order to reveal the love and do the work of God. It is His duty towards the Father, for through it He makes God's goodness visible. Herein also is shown the love of the Father towards Him, that He entrusts Him to accomplish His work in those whom He sends to Him. They are God's gifts to Him. The Father Himself, by giving them to Him, establishes Jesus' messiahship: "He who has the bride, is the bridegroom."[157] And the fact that they come to Jesus is a proof that the Father has already begun His work in them. They are of the truth. Jesus, by accepting them, reveals His love for the Father.[158] By awakening, in those who are of the truth, faith in and love for Him, He "finishes" the Father's work.

Thus, Jesus' love for men is grounded in the love of God. "As the Father hath loved me, so also have I loved you."[159] In these words He not only compares His love for the disciples with God's love for Him, but also expresses the thought that His love for them is *founded* on God's love for Him. He repays this love by loving them. What God gives to Him, He gives to them that are His.

As His love for men has its source solely in God, men's desires do not move Him to action. The people could not force Him to do "signs and wonders" against His will. Even towards His mother

---

[155] The words about self-denial in John 12:25 refer not only to the disciples but also to the Master.

[156] John 9:4.

[157] John 3:29.

[158] John 6:37.

[159] John 15:9.

He maintained His independence.[160] Similarly, at first He leaves the request expressed in John 2:3 unanswered. The same is true of John 7:3. In all these cases it is not mere caprice that rules Him, but each case shows His intense determination only to obey the will of the Father, regardless of how much He was personally moved. His independence from men is rooted in His dependence on God.

Further, Jesus' love for men is independent of their intrinsic worth. Those that the Father has given to be "His own" take on a new transcendent value to the Son; namely, that of being a gift of God: "The good shepherd loveth His sheep because they are His." Therefore, His love for them is not caused by their moral condition. It proceeds out of His own nature and purpose. It is grace: "Him who cometh to Me I shall in no wise cast out" [John 6:37].

The compassion of Jesus for human suffering and need is in no instance a mere emotion, but is always translated into action. His miracles are acts of His all-powerful love, revealing the will of the Father.

All His works, although primarily deeds of love, are "signs" intended to reveal His glory and to awaken men's faith in His Messiahship. In the miracle at Cana, for instance, this is revealed through the gift of joy, which was symbolic of that mystic marriage-joy which is to belong to the Messianic times. The same is true of the feeding of the people in the desert, which also has a Messianic *motif,* the Messiah being the last redeemer, as Moses was the first.[161] In the healing of the blind He reveals Himself as the Light of the World; in the awakening of Lazarus, as the Resurrection and the Life. Thus, His miracles are, in their immediate as well as in their ultimate purpose, a revelation of His love; for the awakening of faith is a higher proof of love than the healing of the sick and the feeding of the hungry.

---

[160] John 2:4.

[161] The traditional Jewish idea of the Messiah being the second Moses (cf. *Numbers Rabbah* 11:2) is also suggested in Acts; cf. 3:22–23, 7:35ff.

All these "works," His εργα [*erga*],[162] He does in the name of the Father.[163] They are the works of God;[164] they come from the Father (John 10:32), for the Father who is in Him works them (John 14:10). They are all *one work* which God gave Him to do (John 17:4). However, although His works bear witness of Him that the Father has sent Him,[165] He prefers the faith which is awakened by His *word* to that which is based on His *works*.[166] His words are spirit and life.[167]

He gives to them His whole πληρωμα ["fullness," *pleroma*]: "of His *fullness* we all received and grace for grace" (John 1:16), which means grace succeeding grace perpetually. All that God has given to Him, He gives to them—His freedom (John 8:36), His peace (John 14:27), His joy (John 15:11), His glory, which the Father gave Him (John 17:22)—and He declares unto them the Father's Name; i.e., His character, "that the love wherewith Thou hast loved Me may be in them, and I in them."[168] As the Messiah, He gives grace and truth (cf. John 1:17 with Micah 7:20). He gives all this by giving Himself. He is the Way, the Truth, and the Life.[169] "He that eateth Me shall live by Me" (John 6:56).

The consummation of His "giving Himself" is His death. It is not only the highest expression of His love, it is its perfection. He loved them εις τελος ["to the end," *eis telos*]; i.e., perfectly.[170]

Jesus, by His love, expects to awaken in men love for Himself and for each other. "If God were your Father you would love Me"

---

[162] This designation is characteristic of the Fourth Gospel; with the exception of Matthew 11:2, it is not found anywhere else in the New Testament.

[163] John 10:25, 4:34, 5:36, 9:3, 10:37.

[164] John 10:32.

[165] Cf. John 5:36, 10:25, 37ff., 15:24.

[166] John 2:23ff., 4:41, 48.

[167] John 6:63, 68.

[168] [John 17:26.]

[169] [John 14:6.]

[170] John 13:1. Cf. for this meaning of the word Luke 18:5; 1 Thessalonians 2:16.

(John 8:42). "If ye love Me" (John 14:15). The whole messianic consciousness of Jesus is expressed in this expectation of love. He seeks not His own glory (John 7:18), but through awakening faith in Himself He awakens faith in God. Thus God Himself is either loved or hated in Him (John 15:23).[171] The world hates Jesus because He reveals its sin. He convinces of sin. The consequence is that those who come in contact with Him either hate *Him* or *themselves*. He whose works are wrought in God, his love Jesus wins; "he cometh to the light" (John 3:21).

It has been rightly observed[172] that "opulent as the New Testament is in the experience and the expression of love, tracing as it does that marvelous river to its fountain-head in Christ, nevertheless, for Christ Himself it has not one fond word, not one endearing phrase." [173] While the apostles readily applied their expressions of endearment to one another, yet with a fine reticence they refrained from applying them to Him. They were conscious of a relationship with Him which was something quite above and apart from their relation with their fellows. In Him they were aware of a passion for them of such a quality that they lost sight of their derivative passion for Him. His love for them was of such a kind as to leave them without a name for the extraordinary response it awakened in their own hearts. It was the very depth of their emotion that made them dumb. They were "but as vessels swept onwards to their haven by an irresistible tide of unfailing love."

The test of true love for Him is love for the brethren. This is His only commandment to His disciples: that those whom the Father has given Him should "all be one, as Thou Father art in Me and I in Thee" (John 17:11, 21–23). It is His ultimate and highest aim. He died in order "to gather together in one the children

---

[171] Cf. *Mechilta* on Exodus 14:31: They proved their faith in God by believing in Moses.

[172] Cuthbert McEvoy, "The New Testament Language of Endearment for the Lord Jesus Christ," *The Expositor* 8th series: 6 (1913): 244–250.

[173] The "beloved" in Ephesians 1:6 expresses the heart of God towards the Messiah. Cf. Isaiah 5:1, 41:8.